Right
Minds

Right Minds

A Sourcebook of American Conservative Thought

Gregory Wolfe

Foreword by William F. Buckley, Jr.

REGNERY BOOKS
Chicago   Washington

Regnery Books is a Division of Regnery Gateway, Inc.
All inquiries concerning this book should be directed to Regnery
Books, 1130 17th Street N.W., Washington, D.C. 20036

Library of Congress Cataloging-in-Publication Data

Wolfe, Gregory.
    Right minds.

    Bibliography: p.
    1. Conservatism—United States—Bibliography. 2. Conservatism—
United States—Societies, etc.—Directories. 3. Conservatism—United
States—Archival resources—United States—Directories.
I. Title.
Z1249.C74W64   1987   [E839.5]   016.3205'2'0973   86-20388
ISBN 0-89526-583-4

For my mother and father

CONTENTS

PART II — Brief Lives of American Conservative Minds

PART III — Current Sources of American Conservative Thought

Acknowledgments

This sourcebook was prepared under the auspices of *National Review,* for the *Educational Reviewer, Inc.* In the course of completing the book, I have relied on many sources, written and personal. I am grateful to all of those who contributed to this project.

Jeffrey Nelligan spent many months doing the initial research and suggesting the scope the sourcebook should take. The work he did provided indispensable help.

I have relied greatly on the resources of the Intercollegiate Studies Institute (ISI). Stephen Krason of ISI made available his own extensive conservative bibliography. Also of great value was the *Free Enterprise Resource Index,* published by the Free Enterprise Institute of the Amway Corporation, Ada, Michigan.

George Nash read and commented on the manuscript and was helpful from the outset. My debt to his scholarship will be obvious. Paul Gottfried, Clyde Wilson, and James Gwartney all brought their scholarly knowledge to bear on the bibliography.

And, of course, the principals of *National Review*—its senior editors, its editor-in-chief and its publisher—have figured in the enterprise from the beginning. Special thanks, however, must go to Dorothy McCartney, for some last-minute help.

I should add a personal note. To my two teachers, Russell Kirk and Gerhart Niemeyer, I owe more than my intellectual formation: they remain for me models of what the Christian man of letters should be.

E. Victor Milione and John F. Lulves, Jr., my co-workers at ISI, have been consistently helpful and encouraging.

And finally, my wife Suzanne, in addition to her other roles, has also been my editor. By integrating the spiritual and practical sides of life, she combines the virtues of Mary *and* Martha.

Gregory Wolfe

FOREWORD

William F. Buckley, Jr.

Begin by admitting that the diligent Gregory Wolfe and the team that helped him to assemble the material between these covers are absolutely certain to have left out at least one favorite book of every reader of this volume, and perhaps even one favorite author of every reader of this volume. It is always so. That problem, in other circumstances, was faced by Roger Starr who is an editorial writer for the *New York Times*. In a recently published book, he announced that every editorial that had appeared in the *New York Times* with which any of the readers of his book disagreed, was not in fact written by him. By the same token, I here disclose that no author, book, or journal not listed or described in this volume was left out by its editor. Samuel Johnson taught us all how to cope with the demand for an explanation into why something was missing (from his Dictionary, in this case): "Ignorance, madam, pure ignorance." And if the Oxford English Dictionary can forget to list a common word ("appendix"), why, so can Mr. Wolfe make an omission.

There is, at the other end, the question of the material included. I am professionally conversant with the literature, but so help me, without the help of this sourcebook I would not have known that there was a book called *The Unaborted Socrates* (Downers Grove, Illinois, InterVarsity Press, 1983): "Using the Socratic debate format, but with a good dose of healthy laughter, this book cuts to the heart of the matter [abortion] and will be especially valuable for young people." I have no doubt that this is so, even as I take solace in not any longer being a young people.

The literature, as here collected, is, well, vast. Mr. Wolfe and his assistants wisely elected to limit it to America-oriented, or America-based, or America-involved persons and books, the alternative being altogether unmanageable as also confusing, given that Spanish conservatism, for instance, intersects our own only here and there, and tends to emphasize different things. What has been collected in the Conservative *Sourcebook* is—let us use a round figure, to allow for the lacunae— ninety percent of anything one would ever need to be familiar with in order to have a full understanding of the many tributaries that flow into the conservative mainstream (how pleasant it is to be able to use the word "mainstream" without being made to sound like a leftwing Republican). The range of books here touched upon, no single reader this side of Erik von Kuehnelt-Leddihn can hope to have mastered in any detail. Already there are students writing about the works of people who have written about the works of Eric Voegelin, or Leo Strauss, or Ludwig von Mises, to name just three of the giants here catalogued. But the context of this book, indeed its mandate, justifies bringing together the large and the small. The small may be a little book, directed at a minor point, but a discrete contribution that might have proved necessary to the evolution of a very large concept. One might even include a little book about the heuristic apple that fell on the head of Isaac Newton.

Now that it is done, one wonders why it was not done before, so obvious are its uses. It might have been done a few years ago, but it could not have been done a generation ago, and this is the most exciting aspect of the *Sourcebook*: the great intellectual energy generated by scholars and journalists (in some cases, both) who, to use the phrase, have stood athwart history, yelling stop.

Mr. Wolfe is to be praised for many things in his arrangement of this volume, for none more than his patient inclusion of the plethora of conservative themes. They are worth enumerating, especially when one reflects that, after the Second World War, the academy was more or less pushing the notion that conservatism had reduced to whatever leverage merchants were left exercising on legislatures to indulge economic exploitation. In those days, the beginning of progressive political history was the inauguration of Franklin Delano Roosevelt. The Communist enterprise was to remind us to be ashamed of our monopoly of nuclear weapons, and if absolutely everything knowable about economics wasn't known, it was only because of the premature death of John Maynard Keynes.

Mr. Wolfe lets the reader curious to know where to turn to come upon the electrically alive bonds that reach back to the Adamses and even to John C. Calhoun. He encourages individual conservatives to speak for themselves in personal testimony. He takes us through a library of effective critiques of modern liberalism. We learn their views (often disparate: Friedrich Hayek and Willmoore Kendall both conservatives? Whigs? Constitutionalists? Traditionalists?—what intrigues, and delights, is that in fact they are properly thought of as companions-in-arms)—their views of government. We deal of course with economics, but also with crime and punishment, and urban problems, and the social sciences, and the environment, sex, the family, the social fabric, race, education, cultural criticism, religion.

And then we are given brief biographies of the principal actors, dead and alive, together with bibliographies of their work, all in lucid, and pleasantly informal language, more in the biographical style than in that of *Who's Who.* And, finally, the *Sourcebook* gives the names of publications, of foundations, and of research centers relevant to a continuing study of conservatism in general, or to any aspect of it.

It is both exciting to leaf through this journal, and exciting to know that it exists. Once upon a time, not so long ago, it was very dark out there. It is now a bustling city, hospitable to thinkers, and poets, and critics, and historians, and economists. Always, of course, there are the street fights, and the decontamination squads need to be called in every now and then; sometimes even there is open warfare, but nothing of Punic proportions as, little by little, what they have in common is a reifying palpability of their brotherhood. It is a very full life, in Conservative City. The music is both lyrical and impassioned, the poetry often airborne, the knowledge profound, responsible, communicable. This is their *Sourcebook,* and this citizen of that community is proud of it.

INTRODUCTION

In the preface to the paperback edition of *The Conservative Intellectual Movement in America Since 1945,* George Nash notes that what in the 1970s was a "substantial" conservative literature has in the 1980s "reached the proportions of . . . a tidal wave." This book is an attempt at taming that tidal wave by culling from it a few clear pools from which the interested reader can drink.

The sheer size of the conservative community, with its numberless think tanks, policy studies, special interest lobbies, journals, even its own colleges, has made it difficult for a noninitiate to wade through the material and discover the central ideas of conservatism. But a second, and perhaps more important, factor in complicating the search for conservative principles has been the seemingly sudden emergence of the Right from a few secluded classrooms and editorial offices to the halls of Congress and the White House itself. Conservatism is now a powerful, ubiquitous political force which has managed to shift the whole political discussion in America to the right. Liberals are calling for balanced budgets and tax cuts; *The New Republic* is sounding more and more like *National Review;* conservative student newspapers are springing up on all the major campuses, including the very citadels of elitist liberalism. Only a few years before, Richard Nixon had justified his interventionist economic policies with the somewhat premature declaration: "We are all Keynesians now." Given the current political climate, it is tempting to claim that "we are all conservatives now."

13

It is a temptation to be resisted. Conservatives know that day-to-day politics exists in a perpetual present tense, much like the fashion world. But truth cannot be acquired by joining a bandwagon. Conservatives believe, in Richard Weaver's phrase, that "ideas have consequences," and that public policy cannot be formed without an adequate knowledge of the accumulated wisdom of the past. There are those in the media and even among those who call themselves conservatives who are ignorant of the American conservative tradition. For example, whereas some journalistic observers may think that "supply-side" economics burst on the scene from nowhere, it actually rests on decades of work done by Ludwig von Mises and the "Austrian" economists, who focus on the concrete valuations and incentives that motivate human action. The neoconservatives, whatever their intellectual accomplishments, have relied heavily on the thought of the conservative political philosopher Leo Strauss and his students.

The point is simply this. Conservatism, while it has necessarily sought political expression, is grounded on principle, not pragmatism. This sourcebook is thus weighted toward ideas—not ideas in the abstract, but as conservatives have developed them in the concrete experiences of American history. Every attempt has been made to include here the intellectual core of conservatism. Though some personal preferences may have crept into the selection of material, I have tried to be as catholic as possible without going beyond the bounds of mainstream conservative thought.

The scope of the book has been restricted to *America,* partly due to space limitations, but also because conservatives have resolutely rejected the liberal contention that there is no conservative tradition in this country. John Adams was expounding the conservative case against ideology several years before Burke began his mature career. The European thinkers listed in this study are there because they have had a particular impact on American conservatives.

The bibliographical section is inevitably top-heavy with post-1945 material so as to be representative of the rapidly growing, sophisticated conservative analysis of liberalism and the paternalistic state. There is some duplication in the entries, but it has been kept to a minimum. In order to make this sourcebook a useful tool and not merely a scholarly work, I have listed the most recent, most readily available editions whenever possible. In putting together sections on such areas as history and literature I realize that the finest works in these subjects should not exhibit a political predilection; the books noted here are those that either support, or are consonant with, a conservative outlook.

The biographical section poses a number of problems. First, there are certain statesmen and thinkers about whom conservatives have been bitterly divided, such as Jefferson and Lincoln. Some of these I have left out, in favor of those figures around whom a consensus has formed. Space limitations have led me to often allow a representative figure to stand for others; thus Hawthorne is included, but Melville, who also possessed conservative insights, is only mentioned in the paragraph about Hawthorne. The post-1945 section is not meant to be a *Who's Who* of contemporary conservatism, but a survey of those writers who have had a significant impact on conservative thought.

With the "current sources" I have looked for the groups and publications representing the central concerns—political, social, and intellectual—of the majority of conservatives. In keeping with the emphasis on ideas, political action groups or party-affiliated organizations have not been included. I have tried to ensure that the listings are accurate and up-to-date, but the reader should be warned that addresses and phone numbers (not to mention the very existence of certain organizations) are liable to frequent change.

Throughout, I have sought to evoke the vigor, persuasiveness, and diversity of conservative thought so that the reader can pursue the subjects that interest him at greater length. At the very least it should be clear that while others have lost themselves in the abstractions of ideology or the pieties of sentimental humanitarianism, conservatives have—with few exceptions—remained in their right minds.

Gregory Wolfe
Intercollegiate Studies Institute
May 1986

Part I — A Bibliography of Conservative Writings

The American Conservative Tradition

Buckley, William F., Jr., ed., *Did You Ever See A Dream Walking? American Conservative Thought in the 20th Century;* Indianapolis, IN, Bobbs Merrill, 1970.
A valuable, comprehensive collection of essays by a diverse group of conservative thinkers, including Burnham, Meyer, Kendall, Hazlitt, Kirk, and Chambers.

Carey, George, ed., *Freedom and Virtue: The Conservative/ Libertarian Debate:* Lanham, MD, University Press of America/Intercollegiate Studies Institute, 1984.
The "debate" has been raging for decades, but it has helped to clarify first principles; here outspoken representatives of each side (Kirk, Walter Berns, Robert Nisbet, Murray Rothbard, Tibor Machan, et al.) slug it out.

Continuity: A Journal of History, No. 4/5 (Spring/Fall 1982) - "Special Issue: Conservatism and History." Bryn Mawr, PA, Intercollegiate Studies Institute.
Scholarly essays relating to historical subjects by Stephen Tonsor, Paul Gottfried, Forrest McDonald, and others.

Chodorov, Frank, *One is a Crowd;* New York, Devin Adair, 1952.
The manifesto of an iconoclastic libertarian who influenced a generation of conservative writers.

Davidson, Donald, *The Attack on Leviathan: Regionalism*

and Nationalism in the United States; Chapel Hill, University of North Carolina Press, 1938.
Davidson's argument antedated the conservative post-war Renaissance, and is an example of the best of traditional Southern thought.

Evans, M. Stanton, *The Future of Conservatism;* New York, Holt Rinehart Winston, 1968.
Somewhat dated now, this volume predicted (in darkest 1968) a conservative resurgence; still contains readable, relevant political analysis.

Goldwater, Barry M., *The Conscience of a Conservative;* Shepardsville, Ky., Victor Publishing Co., 1960.
This broadside sold tens of thousands of copies and galvanized conservative populist support.

Goldwin, Robert, ed., *Left, Right and Center: Essays in Liberalism and Conservatism in the United States;* Chicago, Rand McNally, 1967.
Another readable collection.

Guttman, Allan, *The Conservative Tradition in America;* New York, Oxford University Press, 1967.
An analysis of Conservatism based on the liberal thesis that America's political tradition is solely liberal.

Harbour, William R., *The Foundations of Conservative Thought: An Anglo-American Tradition in Perspective;* Notre Dame, IN, University of Notre Dame Press, 1982.
A balanced, if not inspired, historical account.

Hart, Jeffrey, *The American Dissent: A Decade of Modern Conservatism;* Garden City, NY, Doubleday, 1966.
Hart's book was an attempt to sum up the efforts of the *National Review* circle of writers in its first decade.

Kendall, Willmoore, *The Conservative Affirmation;* Chicago, Henry Regnery, 1985.
A collection of mordant essays and reviews attacking such liberal sacred cows as McCarthyism, the "open society," pacifism, and an activist presidency.

Kirk, Russell, *The Conservative Mind,* seventh ed.; Chicago, Henry Regnery, 1986.
Beyond question, this is the Bible of the conservative intellectual movement; here Kirk provides conservatives with a long and varied intellectual patrimony, beginning with Edmund Burke in England and John Adams in America, and ending with T.S. Eliot. Must reading.

———*A Program for Conservatives;* Chicago, Henry Regnery, 1954.
Expanding on particular themes, such as order, social boredom, community, power, and tradition, Kirk issues a call to action.

———*Reclaiming a Patrimony;* Washington, DC, Heritage Foundation, 1982.
The essays collected here cover a wide range of topics, from collective bargaining and criminal law to historical consciousness and architecture.

———ed., *The Portable Conservative Reader,* New York, Viking Press, 1982.
An excellent companion to Kirk's *The Conservative Mind,* this volume reprints pieces by Burke, Adams, Calhoun, Coleridge, Newman, and many more.

Meyer, Frank S., *The Conservative Mainstream;* New Rochelle, NY, Arlington House, 1969.
In this volume Meyer assembled his spirited "Principles and Heresies" columns from *National Review.*

———*In Defense of Freedom: A Conservative Credo;* Chicago, Henry Regnery, 1962.
An influential work which called for a "fusion" between traditional conservatism and libertarianism; it has been praised and damned, and continues to provoke response.

———ed., *What is Conservatism?;* New York, Holt, Rinehart and Winton, 1964.
Putting his "fusionism" into action, Meyer here brought together various strands of conservatism with essays by Kirk, Hayek, Buckley, Roepke and others.

Modern Age, Vol. 26, Nos. 3-4 (Summer/Fall 1982) — Silver Jubilee Issue: "A Generation of the Intellectual Right." Bryn Mawr, PA, Intercollegiate Studies Institute.
This anniversary issue of "the principal quarterly of the intellectual Right" (Nash) contains memoirs, tributes, plus major essays and reviews by conservative scholars.

Nash, George H., *The Conservative Intellectual Movement in America Since 1945;* New York, Basic Books, 1976.
A masterful intellectual history of the post-war conservative movement, tracing the shifting patterns of thought and bound together by a smooth narrative style. An indispensable book.

Rossiter, Clinton L., *Conservatism in America: The Thankless Persuasion,* revised ed.; New York, Alfred A. Knopf, 1962.
A muddled book by a popularizer; proceed with caution.

Sowell, Thomas, *Dissenting from Liberal Orthodoxy: A Black Scholar Speaks for the "Angry Moderates";* Washington, DC, American Enterprise Institute, 1976.
Sowell, a brilliant economist, represents a new generation of

black scholars and entrepreneurs dissatisfied with liberal paternalism.

Steinfels, Peter, *The Neoconservatives;* New York, Simon and Schuster, 1979.
A somewhat critical and condescending study of Irving Kristol, Norman Podhoretz and Co. by the editor of *Commonweal.*

Weaver, Richard, *Life Without Prejudice and Other Essays;* Chicago, Henry Regnery, 1965.
Among the essays by this seminal conservative thinker are discussions of individualism and of the conservative/libertarian debate.

Whittaker, Robert, ed., *The New Right Papers;* New York, St. Martin's Press, 1982.
More populist and political than the Old Right, the New Right is nevertheless solidly in the conservative tradition, as witness these essays by Rusher, Weyrich, Hart, and their comrades.

Wilson, Francis G., *The Case for Conservatism;* reprinted, Westport, CT, Greenwood Press, 1969.
Thoughtful and lucid, this slim book by an outstanding political scientist helped to form the conservative consensus when it first appeared in 1951.

The Conservative as Witness:
Personal Testimony

Buckley, James, *If Men Were Angels: A View from the Senate;* New York, G.P. Putnam, 1975.
The political opinions and reflections of the Conservative senator from New York from 1971-1977.

Buckley, William F., *God and Man at Yale;* Chicago, Henry Regnery, 1971.
Yale got more than it bargained for when it accepted WFB: this book provoked outrage when it claimed, quite rightly, that the trustees and alumni who thought Yale's students were being taught the value of God and a free economy were sadly mistaken.

——ed., *Odyssey of a Friend: The Letters of Whittaker Chambers to William F. Buckley, Jr., 1954-1961;* New York, G.P. Putnam, 1970.
These letters are witty, often moving accounts of Chambers's deepest convictions.

Chamberlain, John, *A Life With the Printed Word;* Chicago, Henry Regnery, 1981.
The memoirs of a conservative journalist whose style and professional competence have been matched by equally high principles and prejudices.

Chamberlin, William Henry, *The Evolution of a Conservative;* Chicago, Henry Regnery, 1959.
Abandoning his early Communism, Chamberlin went on to develop a defense of American individualism.

Chambers, Whittaker, *Witness;* Chicago, Henry Regnery, 1978.
"One of the most significant autobiographies of the twentieth century," this story of Chambers's period as a Communist agent, his disillusionment, and his subsequent confrontation with Alger Hiss is of more than historical interest: it is a prophetic call to acknowledge the decline of the West and to nourish the "permanent things."

Kristol, Irving, *Reflections of a Neoconservative;* New York, Basic Books, 1983.
An intellectual who has always been at the center of the war of ideas (if not always on the right side) here tells of his move from liberalism to a support of democratic capitalism.

Lyons, Eugene, *Assignment in Utopia;* New York, Greenwood Press, 1971.
The memoir of his period in Moscow, during Stalin's reign of terror in the 1930s, where he discovered that "utopia" means "nowhere."

Morley, Felix, *For the Record;* Chicago, Henry Regnery, 1979.
The founder and editor of *Human Events,* president of Haverford College, and former editor of the *Washington Post* records his life and times.

Nock, Albert Jay, *Memoirs of a Superfluous Man;* Chicago, Henry Regnery, 1964.
Not so much an autobiography as the finely crafted personal reflections of an incisive conservative mind; this volume influenced a generation of post-war conservative writers.

Podhoretz, Norman, *Making It;* New York, Harper & Row, 1980.
Neoconservative editor of *Commentary* recalls the ambitions of the young Jewish intellectuals of his generation.

——*Breaking Ranks;* New York, Harper & Row, 1979.
Podhoretz here tells, with some bitterness and a great deal of passion, of his emergence from the ranks of doctrinaire, urban liberalism.

Regnery, Henry, *Memoirs of a Dissident Publisher;* New York, Harcourt, Brace Jovanovich, 1979.
The leading publisher of conservative works for thirty years, Regnery remembers his authors and their books, from Ezra Pound to Bill Buckley.

Rusher, William, *The Rise of the Right;* New York, Wm. Morrow, 1984.
Partly autobiographical, this work chronicles the conservative renaissance from the founding of *National Review* and the "Draft Goldwater" campaign to Reagan's occupancy of the White House.

Santayana, George, *Persons and Places,* 3 volumes; New York, Scribners, 1944.
Half Spanish Catholic, half Yankee, Santayana brilliantly recollects a faltering and confused era in the history of the West; his urbane and observant mind permeates these volumes.

Toledano, Ralph de, *Lament for a Generation;* New York: Farrar, Straus, Giroux, 1960.
A leftist in the Thirties, Toledano was shocked by the hypocrisy surrounding the Hiss-Chambers trial and became a conservative; this is his autobiography.

The Conservative Critique of Liberalism

Buckley, William F., Jr., *Up From Liberalism: 25th Anniversary Edition;* Briarcliff Manor, NY, Stein & Day, 1985.
Searching critique not only of the contradictions and failures of liberal ideology, but of the conservatism that must be a viable alternative.

Burnham, James, *Suicide of the West;* Chicago, Regnery/Gateway, 1985.
A "systematic analysis and indictment of liberal ideology: its alleged double standard, guilt complex, relativistic theory of truth" and inherent connection to Communism (Nash).

Evans, M. Stanton, *The Liberal Establishment;* New York, Devin-Adair, 1965.
Examining the media, the intellectuals, and the bureaucracy, Evans concludes that liberal control of thought and expression is far advanced, though under the guise of free institutions; still relevant today.

Hayek, Friedrich A., *The Road to Serfdom,* Chicago, University of Chicago Press, 1956.
The Nobel prize-winner's classic argument that government planning inevitably leads to socialist tyranny.

Minogue, Kenneth, *The Liberal Mind;* New York, Random House, 1963.

A professor at the London School of Economics, Minogue here provides an analysis of liberalism that rivals Burnham's in its comprehensiveness.

Strauss, Leo, *Liberalism, Ancient and Modern;* New York, Basic Books, 1968.
A study by one of the finest political philosophers of this century.

Weaver, Richard, *Ideas Have Consequences;* Chicago, University of Chicago Press, 1984.
This seminal work, which traces the decline of Western culture from the medieval nominalist heresy, defies summary, but has become an invaluable weapon in the conservative arsenal.

American Government and Politics

Adams, John, *A Defense of the Constitutions of the United States,* New York, Da Capo, 1971.
A long, rambling work, but one that contains some of the profoundest conservative political and historical analysis by an American; a refutation of the "democratic absolutism" of the French *philosophes.*

Babbitt, Irving, *Democracy and Leadership;* Indianapolis, IN, Liberty Press, 1979.
An attack on naturalism and utilitarianism, Babbitt upholds a moral standard to which true leaders must adhere if society is not to be ruled by unrestrained passions.

Beichman, Arnold, *Nine Lies About America;* La Salle, IL, Open Court, 1972.
A vigorous and witty rebuttal of the cliches promulgated by the New Left about America as an evil empire.

Boorstin, Daniel, *The Genius of American Politics;* Chicago, University of Chicago Press, 1953.
The "genius" is precisely the American people's refusal to follow an ideological program, but rather to rely on experience, tradition, and natural law.

Bradford, M.E., *A Better Guide Than Reason;* La Salle, IL, Sherwood Sugden, 1979.
Bradford examines a number of lesser-known statesmen of the

31

Founding era, and contends that the "lamp of experience" rather than abstract reason guided the framers of the Constitution.

——*A Worthy Company: Brief Lives of the Framers of the United States Constitution;* Marlborough, NH, Plymouth Rock Foundation, 1982.
These sketches include brief biographical introductions followed by concise political evaluations that reflect a thorough knowledge of the period.

Brownson, Orestes, *The American Republic;* New Haven, College and University Press, 1972.
A neglected classic, this nineteenth century work contends that the Constitution can only work if the American people are morally self-governed.

Burnham, James, *Congress and the American Tradition;* Chicago, Henry Regnery, 1965.
The decline of Congress at the hands of the liberal cult of a strong, ideologically motivated Executive branch is here thoroughly documented and evaluated.

Calhoun, John C., *A Disquisition on Government;* New York, Liberal Arts Press, 1953.
The great Southern statesman's case for constitutional, rather than "absolute" democracy.

Cooper, James Fenimore, *The American Democrat;* Indianapolis, IN, Liberty Press, 1981.
While praising democracy's virtues, Cooper stands by the natural aristocracy that must lead a nation, sometimes against the momentary "will of the people."

Diamond, Martin, et al., *The Democratic Republic: An Introduction to American National Government;* Chicago, Rand McNally, 1970.

Unfortunately out of print, this American government textbook is an excellent source for unbiased, meaty material on the American political tradition.

Federalist, The, (Alexander Hamilton, James Madison, John Jay); many editions.
These essays were written to persuade New Yorkers to ratify the Constitution, but they transcend their immediate purpose and remain the central political document in America; they are full of conservative wisdom, mostly forgotten by amnesiac liberals.

Feulner, Edwin J., Jr., *Conservatives Stalk the House: The Story of the Republican Study Committee;* Ottawa, IL, Green Hill, 1983.
The president of the Heritage Foundation recounts the way he and other conservative intellectuals revitalized the RSC and made it a force to be reckoned with on Capitol Hill.

Gentz, Friedrich von, *The Origins and Principles of the American Revolution, Compared with the Origin and Principles of the French Revolution;* Delmar, NY, Scholar's Facsimiles & Reprints, 1977.
This nineteenth century German's work is included because it remains the classic exposition of the American revolution as a "revolution not made but prevented."

Hyneman, Charles, and Lutz, Donald, eds., *American Political Writings During the Founding Era, 1760-1805;* Indianapolis, IN, Liberty Press, 1983.
A superb collection with a helpful introduction.

I'll Take My Stand (John Crowe Ransom, et al.); Baton Rouge, Louisiana State University Press, 1977.
These essays by the "Southern Agrarians" were not merely a defense of agriculture as opposed to industrialism; they were an affirmation of a traditional society threatened by

a utopian liberal progressivism that sought to remake human nature.

Isaac, Rael Jean, and Isaac, Erich, *The Coercive Utopians: Social Deception by America's Power Players;* Chicago, Regnery/Gateway, 1983.
Uncovering the "well-hidden effort of the privileged, well-educated, affluent elite—who believe this country's institutions are evil and oppressive—to change our way of life"; looks into the churches, environmental and peace groups, universities, and the bureaucracy.

Jaffa, Harry, *Crisis of a House Divided;* Garden City, NY, Doubleday, 1959.
A learned and revealing study of the famous Lincoln-Douglas debates.

Kendall, Willmoore and Carey, George, *The Basic Symbols of the American Political Tradition;* Baton Rouge, Louisiana State University Press, 1970.
Contrary to the liberal myth that the Founding Fathers were often too "authoritarian," the American political tradition rests not on abstract "rights" but on "the deliberate sense of the community," whose virtuous representatives seek transcendent truth.

Kilpatrick, James Jackson, *The Sovereign States;* Chicago, Henry Regnery, 1957.
A stalwart defender of the states' rights tradition, Kilpatrick lashes out at the "federalizing" of almost everything by an activist central government.

Kirk, Russell, *The Roots of American Order;* La Salle, IL, Open Court, 1974; now available from Pepperdine University Press, Malibu, CA.

Reaching back to the Greek, Roman, Hebrew, and Christian pillars of American order, Kirk provides a readable narrative that should be on every American's bookshelf.

——*John Randolph of Roanoake;* Indianapolis, IN, Liberty Press, 1978.
The eccentric but eloquent Southern statesman here receives the attention he deserves.

——and James McClellan, *The Political Principles of Robert A. Taft;* New York, Fleet, 1967.
A balanced and appreciative treatment of the much-misunderstood Senator from Ohio who for many years held the conservative banner in the national political sphere.

Kristol, Irving, *On the Democratic Idea in America;* New York, Harper & Row, 1972.
The essays in this volume cover such subjects as pornography, urban issues, foreign policy, and utopianism.

Morgan, Richard E., *Disabling America: The "Rights Industry" in Our Time;* New York, Basic Books, 1984.
Morgan demonstrates that the law relating to civil liberties and "rights" has been manipulated by an ideological elite, with the result that the schools, the churches, the military, and the criminal justice system have been disabled.

Murray, John Courtney, S.J., *We Hold These Truths;* New York, Doubleday Image, 1964.
Murray's argument, that the American political tradition is consonant with the Catholic understanding of natural law, is of importance for non-Catholics, since it denies the myth of a modernist, Lockean America.

Navarro, Peter, *The Policy Game: How Special Interests and Ideologues are Stealing America;* New York, John Wiley, 1984.
A scholarly work showing how the special interest groups have taken advantage of lawmakers' political motivations to ransack the public treasury and twist the law to their desires.

Novak, Michael, *The Spirit of Democratic Capitalism;* New York, Simon & Schuster, 1982.
Novak's thesis is that democratic capitalism is in fact undergirded by moral and theological principles that encourage risk, saving, and creativity, and that these principles have led to unparalleled prosperity and freedom.

Tocqueville, Alexis de, *Democracy in America;* Garden City, NY, Doubleday Anchor, 1969.
The unrivalled study of the American system by the French conservative social thinker.

Weaver, Richard M., *The Southern Tradition at Bay;* New Rochelle, NY, Arlington House, 1968.
A thoughtful and properly "revisionist" study of America's most conservative region.

Political Philosophy

Arendt, Hannah, *On Revolution;* New York, Viking, 1963.
"With nuclear power at a stalemate," writes Arendt, "revolutions have become the principal political factor of our time." Her prophecy and her analysis still ring true.

——*Origins of Totalitarianism;* New York, Harcourt, Brace & World, 1966.
A profound study of the twentieth century's one addition to the forms of government.

Babbitt, Irving, *Democracy and Leadership;* Indianapolis, IN, Liberty Press, 1979.
See under "American government."

Bishirjian, Richard, *A Public Philosophy Reader,* New Rochelle, NY, Arlington House, 1978.
An introductory section on public philosophy by Bishirjian is followed by practitioners of that art, such as Novak, Kristol, Gerhart Niemeyer, Robert Nisbet, and Thomas Molnar.

Burnham, James, *Suicide of the West: The Meaning and Destiny of Liberalism;* Chicago, Regnery/Gateway, 1985.
See under "The Conservative Critique of Liberalism."

Carey, George and Schall, James V., S.J., eds., *Essays on Christianity and Political Philosophy;* Lanham, MD, Univer-

sity Press of America/Intercollegiate Studies Institute, 1984.
Linking these two subjects has not been popular in professional political science circles, but it is done here by Gerhart Niemeyer, James V. Schall, Ellis Sandoz and others.

Germino, Dante, *Beyond Ideology: The Revival of Political Philosophy;* New York, Harper & Row, 1967.
Drawing on the groundbreaking work of Eric Voegelin and Leo Strauss, Germino points to a restoration of political philosophy from its current domination by quantifiers and ideologues.

——*Machiavelli to Marx: Modern Western Political Thought;* Chicago, University of Chicago Press, 1979.
A survey of modern political ideologies.

Hayek, Friedrich von, *The Constitution of Liberty;* Chicago, University of Chicago Press, 1960.
A "positive statement of the principles of a free society" based on the rule of law.

——*The Road to Serfdom;* Chicago, University of Chicago Press, 1956.
See under "The Conservative Critique of Liberalism."

Hoover, Herbert, *The Challenge to Liberty;* 1934; reprinted, New York, Da Capo, 1973.
"Liberty comes alone...where the hard-won rights of men are held unalienable, where governments themselves may not infringe, where governments are indeed but the mechanisms to protect and sustain these liberties. . . ."

Kirk, Russell, *Enemies of the Permanent Things;* La Salle, IL, Sherwood Sugden, 1984.

An examination of moral norms, or the lack of them, in literature and politics.

Lippmann, Walter, *The Public Philosophy;* Boston, Little, Brown, 1965.
While much of Lippmann's writing contains the pious reiteration of liberal sentiments, this book reflects his later turn toward conservatism; it calls for a return to an order undergirded by natural law.

Molnar, Thomas, *Utopia: The Perennial Heresy;* New York, Sheed & Ward, 1967.
Far from being harmless visionaries, utopians (even seemingly benign utopians like Teilhard de Chardin) threaten the existence of civil society because they have abandoned the "Christian realism" which believes in original sin for a false, abstract world.

——*The Decline of the Intellectual;* New Rochelle, NY, Arlington House, 1973.
The "intellectual" has become the purveyor of ideologies which deify man as the creator of society and even of meaning; only the humility of the philosopher, who is open to reality, can eradicate the disease of the mind known as ideology.

Niemeyer, Gerhart, *Between Nothingness and Paradise;* Baton Rouge, Louisiana State University Press, 1971.
Revolutionary thinkers like Marx put forward a "total critique of society" which sees existing reality as completely evil, necessitating its remaking by violence and tyranny; the one "total critique" that is not destructive comes from the transcendent vision of a philosopher like St. Augustine, with his concept of the two cities.

Nozick, Robert, *Anarchy, State, and Utopia;* New York, Basic Books, 1974.

An influential case for a minimal, "nightwatchman" state which has been used by many libertarians.

Oakeshott, Michael, *Rationalism in Politics and Other Essays;* New York, Methuen, 1981.
This British philosopher has lent support to various American conservative thinkers, especially in his concept of the "nomocratic" society (ruled by law and tradition) versus the "teleocratic" society (driven toward a specific ideological "end," such as the rule of the proletariat).

Ryn, Claes G., *Democracy and the Ethical Life;* Baton Rouge, LA, Louisiana State University Press, 1978.
"Constitutional" democracy, based on ethical restraints, is superior to "plebiscitary" democracy, which encourages momentary passions; Ryn here constructs a major refutation of Rousseau's view of man and politics.

Stanlis, Peter, *Edmund Burke and the Natural Law;* Lafayette, LA, Huntington House, 1986.
The first book to demonstrate that Burke's political understanding was guided not merely by experience or tradition, but by the Western concept of natural law as it was developed from Aristotle to Hooker.

Strauss, Leo, *Liberalism, Ancient and Modern;* New York, Basic Books, 1968.
See under "The Conservative Critique of Liberalism."

——*Natural Right and History;* Chicago, University of Chicago Press, 1950.
The profound wisdom of the "ancients" concerning "natural right" (usually known as "natural law") has given way to the "modern" doctrines which are marred by positivism and historicism and which ultimately lead to nihilism.

————*What is Political Philosophy?;* Glencoe, IL, Free Press, 1959.
A collection of essays, including many of Strauss's most important dissections of positivism and historicism.

————and Cropsey, Joseph, eds., *History of Political Philosophy;* Chicago, Rand McNally, 1972.
The contributors to this volume cover the great political thinkers in solid, well-researched essays.

Talmon, J.L., *The Origins of Totalitarian Democracy;* New York, Praeger, 1968.
Shows how the radical individualism and egalitarianism of the thinkers of the French Revolution turned into the collectivism of totalitarian democracy; the relevance of this book to the twentieth century should be obvious.

Vivas, Eliseo, *Contra Marcuse;* New York, Dell, 1971.
An impassioned but scholarly rebuttal of the quasi-Marxist thinker who became a campus cult figure in the 1960s and the darling of liberal intellectuals.

Voegelin, Eric, *The New Science of Politics;* Chicago, University of Chicago Press, 1952.
This book could be said to have launched the modern revival of political theory; it contrasts the classical and Christian vision of the state as the representative of transcendent truth with the modern "gnostic" efforts to concoct "laws of history" and to impose a self-proclaimed utopia on society.

————*Science, Politics, and Gnosticism;* Chicago, Regnery/Gateway, 1968.
Exploring some of the ideas in *The New Science of Politics,* the two essays in this volume discuss "gnosticism" as a substitute religion.

Weaver, Richard, *Ideas Have Consequences;* Chicago, University of Chicago Press, 1984.
See under "The Conservative Critique of Liberalism."

Wilhelmsen, Frederick, *Christianity and Political Philosophy;* Athens, GA, University of Georgia Press, 1978.
Though he is indebted to Strauss and Voegelin, Wilhelmsen here contributes many insights of his own on this central topic.

Communism and Ideology

Barron, John, *KGB: The Secret Work of Soviet Secret Agents;* New York, Bantam, 1974.
One of the more readable and straightforward accounts of Soviet subversion in what is becoming a large and rapidly increasing literature.

Burnham, James, *The Coming Defeat of Communism;* New York, John Day, 1950.
Whether he would agree with this title today notwithstanding, this book is characteristic Burnham: unflinching recognition of the "protracted conflict" and a combination of analysis and pragmatic suggestions.

——*Containment or Liberation?;* New York, John Day, 1953.
Burnham chose the latter; his critique of Kennan's containment policy remains prophetic and thoroughly "relevant."

——*The Web of Subversion;* New York, John Day, 1954.
Using a vast amount of congressional testimony, Burnham holds not only that Communist subversion in the U.S. government threatened American freedom, but that its influence weakened our ability to stem the tide of Communism around the world.

Chambers, Whittaker, *Witness;* Chicago, Regnery/Gateway, 1978.
See under "The Conservative as Witness: Personal Testimony."

Conquest, Robert, *The Great Terror;* New York, Macmillan, 1968.
A chilling history of Stalin's purges by one of the eminent historians of the Soviet Union.

Cranston, Maurice, ed., *Prophetic Politics: Critical Interpretations of the Revolutionary Impulse;* New York, Simon & Schuster, 1970.
Essays on the icons and gurus of the New Left (Che Guevara, Sartre, Marcuse, Frantz Fanon, Black Power, and R.D. Laing) by Cranston, Kenneth Minogue, David Martin, and others.

Hollander, Paul, *Political Pilgrims: Travels of Western Intellectuals to the Soviet Union, China & Cuba;* New York, Oxford University Press, 1981.
Perhaps the most common way to legitimize Communist oppression in the minds of the "educated public" has been the "authentic, personal" accounts of visits to totalitarian regimes by gullible leftist intellectuals; here is a definitive study of this phenomenon.

Huntford, Roland, *The New Totalitarians;* New York, Stein & Day, 1980.
Using Sweden as a case study, Huntford reveals a creeping totalitarianism in the pervasive collectivism that has infected that allegedly enlightened socialist country.

Koestler, Arthur, et al., *The God That Failed;* New York, Harper & Row, 1950.
Though few of the authors of this book could be called conservatives, their reasons for dissociating themselves from active participation in the Communist Party have had an enduring effect in many intellectual circles; the contributors include Arthur Koestler, Ignazio Silone, Stephen Spender, and André Gide.

Kuehnelt-Leddihn, Erik von, *Leftism: From De Sade and Marx to Hitler and Marcuse;* New Rochelle, NY, Arlington House, 1974.
A wide-ranging study of leftism that claims: "the vast majority of the leftist ideologies now dominating...most of the modern world are *competitors* rather than *enemies"*; Hitler and fascism are shown to be socialist in origin, and the book concludes with analyses of current policy debates.

Leys, Simon, *Chinese Shadows;* New York, Viking Press, 1974.
Haunting portrayal of the devastation of Chinese culture by Communist totalitarianism.

Lyons, Eugene, *The Red Decade: The Stalinist Penetration of America;* Indianapolis, IN, Bobbs-Merrill, 1941.
One of the earliest attacks on the liberal defenders of Stalin.

Mosher, Stephen, *Broken Earth: The Rural Chinese;* New York, Free Press, 1983.
As an exchange scholar, Mosher was able to observe Chinese rural life directly, and his account of the agricultural, political, and sexual policies of the Communist leadership provide a tragic update on China's woes.

Niemeyer, Gerhart, *An Inquiry into the Soviet Mentality;* New York, Praeger, 1956.
Unaffected by the half-truth that "no one in the Soviet Union believes in Communism any more," Niemeyer investigates the role of ideology in the thinking and structure of Soviet society.

——*The Communist Ideology;* Washington, DC, Government Printing Office, 1959.
A brief, but detailed interpretation of the relation of Communist ideology to political action.

——*Deceitful Peace: A New Look at the Soviet Threat;* New Rochelle, NY, Arlington House, 1971.

At the outset of the era of "detente," Niemeyer told the ugly truth.

Pipes, Richard, *Survival is Not Enough;* New York, Simon & Schuster, 1984.

Hard-headed conclusions from the Harvard Sovietologist and sometime member of the National Security Council.

Sterling, Claire, *The Terror Network: The Secret War of International Terrorism;* New York, Holt, Rinehart & Winston/Reader's Digest Press, 1981.

As training ground and facilitator, Sterling calls the Soviet Union the "beneficiary" of international terrorism: "In effect, the Soviet Union had simply laid a loaded gun on the table leaving others to get on with it." Sterling's narrative charts that activity around the globe.

Strausz-Hupé, Robert, et al., *The Protracted Conflict;* New York, Harper & Row, 1959.

A classic, this book "was intended to provide an analysis of the operational code whereby the international Communist movement carries on conflict in an environment of unrelenting systemic change—or, put differently, a study of how the Communist 'scavengers of revolution' endeavor to make history work for themselves and against the West."

Turner, Robert, *Vietnamese Communism: Its Origins and Development;* Stanford, CA, Hoover Institution Press, 1975.

The definitive work, dispelling myths such as Ho Chi Minh's "nationalism," and providing a detailed history of the Vietnamese Communist Party and numerous comparisons with China and Indochina.

International Relations and Foreign Policy

Beilenson, Laurence, B., *Survival and Peace in a Nuclear Age;* Chicago, Regnery/Gateway, 1980.

"The two underlying basics of our affairs abroad are: Swift further advances in weapons are to be expected; a significant alteration in the nature of men or nations is not to be expected." Among the many persuasive arguments in this book is a case for a full-scale Civil Defense system.

Crozier, Brian, Middleton, Drew, and Murray-Brown, Jeremy, *This War Called Peace;* New York, Universe Books, 1985.

"In totalitarian terms, the only dialogue possible is between an executioner and his victim." So the authors contend in this sweeping historical study which lays to rest the myth of "peaceful coexistence."

Eidelberg, Paul, *Beyond Detente: Toward An American Foreign Policy;* La Salle, IL, Sherwood Sugden, 1977.

Using the statesmanship of the Founding Fathers as his source of first principles, Eidelberg attempts to transcend the twin fallacies of "moralism" and "pragmatism" in order to derive a truly realistic and fully ethical foreign policy.

Falcoff, Mark and Royal, Robert, eds., *Crisis and Opportunity: U.S. Policy in Central America and the Caribbean;* Washington, Ethics & Public Policy Center, DC, 1984.

Thirty essays by "statesmen, scholars, religious leaders, and journalists" make up this balanced volume which is divided into three sections: "Regional and Global Perspectives," "The Struggle in El Salvador," and "Nicaragua: What Kind of Revolution?"

Francis, Samuel, *Soviet Strategy of Terror;* Washington, DC, Heritage Foundation, 1981.
The evidence for the link between the Soviet Union and global terrorism is presented, along with the "infrastructure of terror," plus an extremely important section placing terrorism within the ideological and political objectives of Marxist-Leninist thought.

Graham, Daniel, *High Frontier: A New National Strategy;* Washington, DC, Heritage Foundation, 1982.
One of the first and best proposals for abandoning the doctrine of "Mutual Assured Destruction" for a defense that deters *and* protects.

Gray, Colin, *The Soviet-American Arms Race;* Lexington, MA, Lexington Books, 1976.
A scholarly study that puts this emotionally-loaded issue into factual perspective.

Kelly, J.B., *Arabia, the Gulf and the West: A Critical View of the Arabs and Their Oil Policy;* New York, Basic Books, 1980.
A Middle East expert meticulously unravels the confusions of those who would embrace the Arab cause, and particularly the Saudis, without reservations; full justice is done to this complex part of the world.

Kirkpatrick, Jeane J., *Dictatorship and Double Standards: Rationalism and Reason in Politics;* New York, Simon & Schuster/American Enterprise Institute, 1982.
America's "iron lady" of foreign policy, Dr. Kirkpatrick criticizes the liberal tendency to abstract from history and cul-

tural identity when making sweeping, moralistic judgments in the area of international affairs.

Lawler, Philip F., ed., *Justice and War in the Nuclear Age;* Lanham, MD, University Press of America, 1983.
Among the contributors: then bishop John J. O'Connor, Angelo Codevilla, and James V. Schall; among the topics: "The Intellectual Origins of the Peace Movement," "The Amorality of Arms Control," and "Justice, War and Active Defense."

Lefever, Ernest W., *Amsterdam to Nairobi: The World Council of Churches and the Third World;* Washington, DC, Ethics and Public Policy Center, 1979.
In the space of a few months in 1978, the WCC had given over $200,000 to revolutionary terrorists in southern Africa; Lefever chronicles the radicalizing of this once-respected organization.

——and Hunt, E. Stephen, *The Apocalyptic Premise: Nuclear Arms Debated;* Washington, DC, Ethics and Public Policy Center, 1982.
The essays in this volume seek to place the nuclear arms debate on a rational basis, not on one which starts from an "apocalyptic premise."

Luttwak, Edward N., *The Grand Strategy of the Soviet Union;* New York, St. Martin's, 1983.
Luttwak contends that the Soviet Union, after a series of ideological, political, and economic failures, is no longer "Lenin's creation," but once again a great military empire driven by the need to expand in order to cover its other failures.

Novak, Michael, "Moral Clarity in a Nuclear Age," *National Review,* April 1, 1983.

The editors at *National Review* devoted an entire issue to this essay alone; William F. Buckley, Jr. has called it "a document that, in virtue of rigorous thought, plain language, and eloquent moral reasoning, cannot fail to achieve ethical consequence."

Pipes, Richard, *Survival is Not Enough: Soviet Realities and America's Future;* New York, Simon & Schuster, 1984.
See under "Communism and Ideology."

———*U.S.-Soviet Relations in the Era of Detente: A Tragedy of Errors;* Boulder, CO, Westview, 1981.
Pipes remained one of the few outspoken critics of "detente" throughout the 1970s; here are his conclusions about that era.

Podhoretz, Norman, *The Present Danger;* New York, Simon & Schuster, 1980.
"Do we have the will to reverse the decline of American power?" Podhoretz asks, warning that if we do not, the "Finlandization of America"—an economic and political subjection to the dictates of Moscow—is bound to follow.

Scott, Otto, *The Other End of the Lifeboat;* Chicago, Regnery Books, 1985.
A sober, historically-minded study of South Africa, its policies, its potential for progress, and its value to the West; a great deal of personal research, travel, and investigation went into the making of this book.

Staar, Richard F., ed., *Arms Control: Myth Versus Reality;* Stanford, CA, Hoover Institution Press, 1984.
A collection of essays stressing that arms control has become a political circus, but also applying realistic principles to their structure and usefulness.

Thompson, W. Scott, ed., *National Security in the 1980s: From Weakness to Strength;* San Francisco, Institute for Contemporary Studies, 1980.
Another valuable collection.

Turner, Robert, *The War Powers Resolution;* Philadelphia, Foreign Policy Research Institute, 1983.
Theoretically flawed, unworkable, and probably unconstitutional: these are Turner's conclusions about Congress's post-Vietnam legislative handcuffs on the president.

Ulam, Adam, *Expansion & Coexistence: Soviet Foreign Policy, 1917 to 1973;* New York, Holt, Rinehart & Winston, 1974.
A clear, unbiased historical survey.

——*The Rivals: America & Russia Since World War II;* New York, Penguin, 1972.
More of the same, covering the period from the Cold War to detente.

Economics

Bauer, P.T., *Equality, the Third World, and Economic Delusion;* Cambridge, MA, Harvard University Press, 1981.
The leading conservative scholar on the subject of "development economics," Bauer has been an indefatigable foe of foreign aid as international welfare; only the market can lift backward nations out of their poverty.

——*Reality and Rhetoric: Studies in the Economics of Development;* Cambridge, MA, Harvard University Press, 1984.
More scholarly polemics on Third World "aid."

Brookes, Warren T., *The Economy in Mind;* New York, Universe Books, 1982.
A columnist for the *Boston Herald-American,* Brookes, like Tom Bethell, has become one of the most lucid, common-sensical writers on economics from a "supply-side" perspective in America today; like all the best supply-side writing, this book emphasizes the human factor, the freedom and creativity of mind and spirit, in economics.

Brozen, Yale, *Concentration, Mergers, and Public Policy;* New York, Macmillan, 1982.
The myths of monopoly and antitrust legislation are here demolished; most of the monopolies in recent times have, in fact, been created by government.

Buchanan, James M., *The Limits of Liberty: Between Anarchy and Leviathan;* Chicago, University of Chicago Press, 1977.
A leading economist of the "public choice" school defends the free economy.

——and Tullock, Gordon, *The Calculus of Consent: Logical Foundations of Constitutional Democracy;* Ann Arbor, MI, University of Michigan Press, 1962.
This is a central document in the development of "public choice" economics: the nature of modern democracy, the egalitarian impetus, and the political calculations of politicians who seek re-election are all taken into account in this new brand of "political economy."

——and Wagner, Richard E., *Democracy in Deficit: The Political Legacy of Lord Keynes;* New York, Academic Press, 1977.
A thorough analysis of the way Keynesianism leads democracies into living beyond their means.

Chamberlain, John, *The Roots of Capitalism;* Indianapolis, IN, Liberty Press, 1976.
Examining both the ideas that led to the growth of a free economy and the copious fruits of that freedom, Chamberlain has produced a readable and compelling defense of capitalism.

——*The Enterprising Americans: A Business History of the United States;* New York, Harper & Row, 1963.
A history of American entrepreneurial energies that eschews trite generalizations, such as the obligatory blanket condemnations of the "robber barons," and charts a neglected but crucial aspect of our national life.

Davenport, John, *The U.S. Economy;* Chicago, Henry Regnery, 1964.

Along with Chamberlain's *The Roots of Capitalism* and Hazlitt's *Economics in One Lesson,* this is unquestionably one of the best primers on democratic capitalism.

Dietze, Gottfried, *In Defense of Property;* Baltimore, Johns Hopkins, 1971.
"The thesis of this book...is that a disregard for private property leads to an erosion of law and order"; a scholarly critique of the theory of "rights" that has brought on property-destroying social legislation.

Fink, Richard H., ed., *Supply-Side Economics: A Critical Appraisal;* Frederick, MD, University Publications of America, 1982.
Essays by many of the leading supply-siders defining the nature of their economic insights as well as arguments by opponents.

Friedman, Milton, *Capitalism and Freedom;* Chicago, University of Chicago Press, 1962.
Friedman's classic blast against the self-defeating attempts of government to manipulate the myriad decisions of the marketplace; economic freedom, he says, is inextricably linked to political freedom.

——*An Economist's Protest;* Englewood Cliffs, NJ, Prentice Hall, 1972.
A collection of Friedman's *Newsweek* columns, all bursting with his brisk, no-nonsense style and policy proposals.

——and Friedman, Rose, *Free to Choose: A Personal Statement;* New York, Harcourt, Brace, Jovanovich, 1980.
A companion to the TV series of the same name, and the best antidote to J.K. Galbraith's socialist TV series, "The Age of Uncertainty"; straight talk about the decline and fall of the welfare state.

——and Schwartz, Anna, *A Monetary History of the United States;* Princeton, Princeton University Press, 1963.
Perhaps the most persistent myth about capitalism is that of the "business cycle" of boom and bust, of which the Great Depression is said to be the "classic" example; this seminal study demonstrated that it was in fact the Federal Reserve Board's mismanagement that partly created and largely sustained the Depression.

Gilder, George, *Wealth and Poverty;* New York, Basic Books, 1981.
Gilder's rhetoric at times approaches the mystical, but this "theology of capitalism" makes the central point that risk, thrift, faith, and morality undergird the creative power of the free economy; this is the philosophical work which complements supply-side economics.

Goodman, John, ed., *Privatization;* Dallas, TX: National Center for Policy Analysis, 1985.
A collection of essays on a creative policy initiative that has already had considerable success in Britain: privatization can mean either the selling off of government-owned entities (like Amtrak), or the contracting out of government services (like sanitation), to the private sector. The results are efficiency and smaller burdens on government budgets and taxpayer's pockets.

Gwartney, James and Stroup, Richard, *Economics: Public and Private Choice,* 3rd ed.; New York, Academic Press, 1980.
Without question the best college economics textbook, written from a free market perspective; it is one of the best-selling texts and would be a valuable reference work for the layman.

Hayek, Friedrich von, *Individualism and Economic Order;* Chicago, University of Chicago Press, 1948.

The speeches and articles gathered here are all related to Hayek's thesis that the innumerable decisions made every day in the marketplace cannot be replaced by a central government, which cannot possibly possess the information exchanged among so many specific buyers and sellers.

——*The Road to Serfdom;* Chicago, University of Chicago Press, 1944.
See under "The Conservative Critique of Liberalism."

Hazlitt, Henry, *Economics in One Lesson;* New Rochelle, NY, Arlington House, 1979.
The lesson is simple, but that hasn't prevented it from being ignored by generations of bureaucrats and politicians: the consequences of an intervention into the market must take into account the long-run effects on the whole of the population; the short-term tinkering of liberals has brought on chaos and ever more frantic attempts at controlling the confusion they have inflicted on the nation.

——*The Failure of the "New Economics";* Princeton, Van Nostrand, 1959.
Practically a point-by-point refutation of Keynes's *General Theory* that remains the definitive study.

——ed., *The Critics of Keynesian Economics;* New Rochelle, NY, Arlington House, 1977.
Essays by economists from John Stuart Mill to Hayek, von Mises, and Hutt.

Hessen, Robert, *In Defense of the Corporation;* Stanford, CA, Hoover Institution Press, 1979.
Taking on the taunts of ideologues like Ralph Nader, Hessen rebuts typical beliefs such as: corporations victimize shareholders, crush smaller competitors, overcharge consumers, and gain special protection from government; a lively, non-technical book.

Hutt, William H., *The Strike-Threat System: The Economic Consequences of Collective Bargaining;* New Rochelle, NY, Arlington House, 1973.
The South African economist argues that while the power to strike can redistribute income in favor of the strikers, it cannot redistribute income in favor of labor in general at the expense of capital in general; moreover, "fear of strikes inflicts far greater damage on the economic system than actual strikes."

——*The Theory of Idle Resources;* Indianapolis, IN, Liberty Press, 1977.
First published in 1939, this attack on Keynes's concept of un-employment has been reprinted and updated with new material by the author.

Kirzner, Israel M., *Competition and Entrepreneurship;* Chicago, University of Chicago Press, 1978.
A sophisticated analysis of real-world, as opposed to the text-book "perfect" competition, proving that the ability of entrepreneurs to enter markets is not as easily closed off as critics believe.

——*The Economic Point of View: An Essay in the History of Economic Thought;* New York, New York University Press, 1976.
Some healthy "revisonist" economic history.

Kristol, Irving, *Two Cheers for Capitalism;* New York, Basic Books, 1978.
The neoconservative Kristol won't claim that capitalism is the product of an inherently moral approach, but he says that it is the best system for meeting human needs, that it does not entail a pronounced lack of "social justice," and he deftly refutes the trendy attacks on "big business."

Lepage, Henri, *Tomorrow, Capitalism: The Economics of Economic Freedom;* La Salle, IL, Open Court, 1978.
"The first popular account of the American revolution in economics," this book has been a best-seller in France and Sweden, a sure indication of its persuasive and prophetic power.

McKenzie, Richard B., *Bound to Be Free;* Stanford, CA, Hoover Institution Press, 1982.
"The case for a free economy is largely a case for freedom in general," concludes this articulate member of a younger generation of free market economists.

Mises, Ludwig von, *Bureaucracy;* Cedar Falls, IA, Center for Future's Education, 1983.
Written near the end of World War II, this warning about the centralization and politicization of society reads as if it were written yesterday by someone trying to understand why Ronald Reagan hasn't made much of a dent in the vast machinery of the federal bureaucracy.

———*A Critique of Interventionism;* New Rochelle, NY, Arlington House, 1977.
Mises believed that those who start in the "middle of the road" inevitably end up on the left; the six essays here contend that an interventionist society is a socialist society.

———*Human Action;* 3rd rev. ed., Chicago, Henry Regnery, 1966.
This fat tome is not summer reading, but it is Mises's masterpiece: the thrust of his interpretation is that an economy is not a machine which is controllable and predictable, but the sum total of human choices and valuations; this thesis has resurfaced in the supply-side theorists.

——*Omnipotent Government;* New Haven, Yale University Press, 1969.

The massive centralization of government during the Second World War did not evaporate at the cessation of hostilities; Mises foresaw the dangers of looking to collectivist solutions and issued this cautionary work.

——*Socialism;* Indianapolis, IN, Liberty Press, 1981.

Hayek once said of *Socialism:* "To none of us young men who read the book when it appeared [1922] was the world ever the same again"; in his Foreword to this edition, Hayek says it "has more immediate application to contemporary events than when it first appeared."

North, Douglas C., and Thomas, Robert Paul, *The Rise of the Western World: A New Economic History;* Cambridge, Cambridge University Press, 1973.

A basic historical survey unbiased against capitalism.

Novak, Michael, *The Spirit of Democratic Capitalism;* New York, Simon & Schuster, 1982.

See under "American Government and Politics."

Nutter, G. Warren, *Political Economy and Freedom;* Indianapolis, IN, Liberty Press, 1983.

Three areas of public policy are discussed in this lively collection of essays: regulation and economic "planning"; the Soviet economic system and our relation to it; and international trade and foreign policy.

Roberts, Paul Craig, *The Supply-Side Revolution: An Insider's Account of Policymaking in Washington;* Cambridge, MA, Harvard University Press, 1984.

Roberts, former Assistant Secretary of the Treasury for Economic Policy from 1981-1982, tells of his efforts to preserve President Reagan's supply-side economic program against pragmatists and self-interested bureaucrats; contains not only a revealing portrait of Washington politics, but an articulate case for the supply-side cause.

Roepke, Wilhelm, *Economics of the Free Society;* Chicago, Henry Regnery, 1963.
Classic defense of the free economy by the German economist who, as an adviser to Ludwig Erhard, was largely responsible for Germany's "economic miracle" after World War II.

——*The Humane Economy: The Social Framework of the Free Market;* Chicago, Henry Regnery, 1960.
Capitalism can only arise when certain moral and spiritual values are practiced; Roepke relates those values to the marketplace and demonstrates that chronic inflation and massive centralization of power are the result of the decline of morality.

Schuettinger, Robert L. and Butler, Eamonn F., *Forty Centuries of Wage and Price Controls;* Washington, DC, Heritage Foundation, 1979.
From the Code of Hammurabi to Nixon's Phase II, the authors document the repeated long-term failures of wage and price controls as a measure against inflation; since inflation is caused by excessive government money-production over national productivity, controls are ill-conceived.

Schumpeter, Joseph, *Capitalism, Socialism, and Democracy;* New York, Harper & Row, 1962.
Schumpeter was an outstanding academic proponent of capitalism when it was far from fashionable; this book includes his pessimistic thesis that capitalism carries the seeds of its own destruction because its very success undermines the conditions for its continued existence.

Sowell, Thomas, *Race and Economics;* New York, D. McKay, 1975.
Sowell, a prolific scholar, has written extensively on the detrimental effects on minorities of extensive government programs; this is an early and extensive study.

——*Knowledge and Decisions;* New York, Basic Books, 1979.
Like Hayek, Sowell delves into the way knowledge and decisions are communicated in the complex process of the marketplace in this work of economic theory.

——*Marxism: Philosophy and Economics;* New York, William Morrow, 1985.
Links Marxist philosophy to its economics and details the debilitating economic fallacies of the system.

Stigler, George, *The Intellectual and the Marketplace;* Glencoe, NY, Free Press, 1963.
Essays by a renowned member of the Chicago school of economics.

——*The Economist as Preacher and other Essays;* Chicago, University of Chicago Press, 1982.
More of the same.

Tullock, Gordon, *The Politics of Bureaucracy;* Washington, DC, Public Affairs Press, 1964.
A "public choice" school economist on the origins of red tape.

Van den Haag, Ernest, ed., *Capitalism: Sources of Hostility;* New Rochelle, NY, Epoch Books/Arlington House, 1979.
The contributors to this volume delve into the psychological factors that lead to an anti-capitalist mentality; they include van den Haag, Stanley Rothman, Peter Bauer, and Lewis Feuer.

The Welfare State

Anderson, Martin, *Welfare: The Political Economy of Welfare Reform in the United States;* Stanford, CA, Hoover Institution Press, 1978.

A vital contribution to the debate over welfare policy; Anderson examines, among other things, the high marginal tax rates that make a wall over which the "underclass" cannot climb, and the evidence that poverty has been virtually eliminated; he concludes that full-scale reform is politically impossible.

Anderson, Terry and Hill, P.J., *The Birth of A Transfer Society;* Stanford, CA, Hoover Institution Press, 1980.

The decisons of the Supreme Court in this century have significantly weakened private property and paved the way for the transfer society; the rights of individuals have been curtailed by bloated government programs.

Blum, Walter, and Kalben, Harvey, Jr., *The Uneasy Case for Progressive Taxation;* Chicago, University of Chicago Press, 1953.

A little-known work, but one which contains many of the strongest arguments against progressivity in taxation; especially interesting in the light of President Reagan's attempts at tax reform.

Freeman, Roger, *The Wayward Welfare State;* Stanford, CA, Hoover Institution Press, 1981.

Throwing money at poverty and social problems, the modus operandi of the Great Society, is here revealed, with the use of cost/benefit analysis, to be a fatuous and self-defeating policy.

Gilder, George, *Wealth and Poverty;* New York, Basic Books, 1981.
See under "Economics."

Hazlitt, Henry, *The Conquest of Poverty;* New Rochelle, NY Arlington House, 1973.
"The history of poverty is almost the history of mankind," writes Hazlitt; the relatively recent phenomenon of a free market system changed all that.

Jouvenel, Bertrand de, *The Ethics of Redistribution;* Cambridge, Cambridge University Press, 1952.
More a work of political science than economics, this work by the great French social theorist explores the philosophical roots of welfarism.

Moynihan, Daniel P., *Maximum Feasible Misunderstanding;* New York, Free Press, 1969.
A tough critique of the failure of the War on Poverty; the liberals behind the "war" were without clear ideas as to the effect of their policies; they "underestimate difficulties, overpromise results, and avoid any evidence of incompatibility and conflict."

Murray, Charles, *Losing Ground: American Social Policy, 1950-1980;* New York, Basic Books, 1984.
The thesis of this definitive work is that the social programs of the last two decades actually slowed down the earlier progress in reducing crime, poverty, ignorance, and discrimination; thoroughly documented, this book has already provoked controversy.

Nozick, Robert, *Anarchy, State, and Utopia;* New York, Basic Books, 1974.
See under "Political Philosophy."

Sowell, Thomas, *Markets and Minorities;* New York, Basic Books, 1982.
The road up for minorities is not welfarism but the free market; discrimination does not explain all differences in economic and social levels, and more government intervention will only retard minority advancement.

Tullock, Gordon, *The Economics of Income Redistribution;* Boston, Kluwer-Nijhoff, 1983.
Scholarly, in-depth investigation of the transfer society.

Williams, Walter, *The State Against Blacks;* New York, New Press, 1982.
Using minimum wage laws, union policies, and bureaucratic regulations, Williams makes a powerful case that the "rules of the game" work to maintain blacks in poverty.

Population, Resources, and the Environment

Baden, John and Stroup, Richard, eds., *Bureaucracy vs. Environment: The Environmental Costs of Bureaucratic Governance;* Ann Arbor, MI, University of Michigan Press, 1981.
Citing ample evidence indicating that bureaucratic fiats have often deterred conservation and anti-pollution measures, the authors point to the self-regulating aspects of the market and argue for prudent, non-ideological laws.

Frieden, Bernard J., *The Environmental Protection Hustle;* Cambridge, MA, Harvard University Press, 1979.
A polemic against the well-funded, ideological environmentalists who have increasingly opposed urban and suburban growth in a fanatic and nearly totalitarian manner.

McCracken, Samuel, *The War Against the Atom;* New York, Basic Books, 1982.
The nuclear energy industry has been crippled by environmentalists, muddled bureaucrats, and bad planning by corporate and local officials; this book defends atomic energy against its ideological foes.

Simon, Julian L., *The Ultimate Resource;* Princeton, Princeton University Press, 1981.
The "ultimate resource" is, of course, the creativity of the human spirit; Simon's comprehensive rebuttal of the doomsayers includes the following assertions: natural resources

and energy are getting less scarce; pollution in the U.S. has been decreasing; the world's food supply is improving; and population growth has long-term benefits.

——and Kahn, Herman, eds., *The Resourceful Earth: A Response to Global 2000;* New York, Basil Blackwell, 1984.
The Global 2000 report put out under President Carter was based on faulty evidence and drew unwarrented conclusions, according to the contributors to this hefty work, who respond in detail in a vast number of specific fields, from population growth to forestry.

Stroup, Richard L. and Baden, John A., *Natural Resources: Bureaucratic Myths and Environmental Management;* Cambridge, MA, Ballinger Publishing Co., 1983.
Just as the marketplace, with its price system, is a self-regulating entity, so the institution of private property functions as an admirable check to greed and rapaciousness, despite the myths propounded by the left.

Tucker, William, *Progress and Privilege: America in the Age of Environmentalism;* Garden City, NY, Doubleday Anchor, 1982.
Tucker's startling contention is that environmentalism has become "the conservatism of the liberals"; he sees the environmentalist movement as dominated by the upper-middle class, East coast elite; he goes on to evaluate the current situation in a lucid, unbiased manner.

Truluck, Phillip N., ed., *Private Rights and Public Lands;* Washington, DC, Heritage Foundation, 1983.
Essays by constitutionalist Bernard Siegan, Senator Steven Symms, economist John Baden, and others.

Law, the Courts and the Constitution

Anastaplo, George, *The Constitutionalist: Notes on the First Amendment*; Dallas, Southern Methodist University Press, 1971.
A conservative constitutional scholar puts this most abused of amendments into historical and philosophical perspective.

Berger, Raoul, *Government by Judiciary: The Transformation of the Fourteenth Amendment*; Cambridge, MA, Harvard University Press, 1977.
The Fourteenth Amendment, passed after the Civil War as a repudiation of slavery, has undergone a strange transformation whereby its "due process" and "equal protection" clauses have been "read into" the Bill of Rights; the result is that federal courts have taken upon themselves a crusade to legislate even the most trivial matters that were previously left to the states, all in the name of high-sounding constitutional phrases. This book, by a legal scholar who is not a conservative, will tell you how this came about.

Berns, Walter, *Freedom, Virtue and the First Amendment*; Chicago, Henry Regnery, 1965.
A "powerful challenge to the liberal interpretation of the First Amendment" (Nash); against the modern, liberal belief in "freedom" as an absolute value, Berns upholds virtue and the state's role in inculcating virtue in its citizens.

69

Bickel, Alexander M., *The Supreme Court and the Idea of Progress*; New Haven, CT, Yale University Press, 1978.
Written by a liberal, this book contains a number of severe indictments of the major decisions of the Warren Court.

Blackstone, Sir William, *Commentaries on the Laws of England*; Chicago, University of Chicago Press, 1979.
Though American legal scholars can pompously say that we have never had a "common law" like that of England, in practice America looked to that tradition; Blackstone's commentary was on the best-seller list in the Founding era for many years.

Bozell, L. Brent, *The Warren Revolution*; New Rochelle, NY, Arlington House, 1966.
The U.S. has "two constitutions": the formal document of 1787 and the unwritten, "fluid" version developed by compromise and consensus; the balance between the two was upset by the 1954 *Brown* decision and subsequent rulings, which arrogated to the Court the sole right to expound and determine the Constitution's meaning.

Canavan, Francis, *Freedom of Expression: Purpose as Limit*; Durham, NC, Carolina Academic Press, 1985.
The subtitle is the book's thesis; liberals have become so dominated by relativism that they must include treason and obscenity in "protected" speech.

Clor, Harry, *Obscenity and Public Morality*; Chicago, University of Chicago Press, 1969.
Opposed to radical libertarian ideas on pornography, Clor advocates a prudent form of censorship.

Corwin, Edwin S., *Court Over Constitution*; Princeton, Princeton University Press, 1938.
The brilliant constitutional scholar issued this early warning signal in 1938!

———*The "Higher Law" Background of American Constitutional Law*; Ithaca, NY, Cornell University Press, 1955.

According to one reviewer: "a vivid portrayal of the two-thousand-year background of natural law thinking that contributed to the character of American law . . . [Corwin traces] the conception of law as basically something to be found rather than made . . . ."

Epstein, Richard, *Takings: Private Property and the Power of Eminent Domain*; Cambridge, MA: Harvard University Press, 1986.

Epstein, a legal scholar at the University of Chicago, here argues convincingly against recent judicial rulings that threaten the central role private property plays in the American political order.

Goldberg, George, *Reconsecrating America*; Grand Rapids, MI, Eerdmans, 1984.

An eloquent Jewish lawyer disentangles the Supreme Court's muddled rulings on church and state and makes common sense proposals for how to restore a reasonable interpenetration of the two.

Kurland, Philip, *Politics, the Constitution and the Warren Court*; Chicago, University of Chicago Press, 1970.

A learned critique of the "politicization" of the Court, by which Kurland means "that the Court's function is no longer primarily the judicial one of resolving legal controversies . . . but the legislative one of making general governmental policies for the nation . . . ."

McGuigan, Patrick B., and Rader, Randell R., eds., *A Blueprint for Judicial Reform*; Washington, DC, Free Congress Research & Education Foundation, 1981.

Thoughtful, practical ways to get us out of the current judicial morass by several leading conservative legal thinkers.

Siegan, Bernard, *Economic Liberties and the Constitution*; Chicago, University of Chicago Press, 1980.
The Supreme Court has indulged in a double standard with regard to civil liberties by refusing to consider administrative and congressional infringements on economic liberty as constitutional violations of civil liberties.

Story, Joseph, *Commentaries on the Constitution*; Boston, Little, Brown, 1873.
Story influenced generations of lawyers by his magisterial defense of the "higher" or natural law foundations of the common law.

Crime and Punishment

Berns, Walter, *For Capital Punishment*; New York, Basic
    Books, 1979.
Like all Berns's books, this one is thoroughly reasoned, and
    reaches beyond the modern mindset to the wisdom of
    the great philosophers and statesmen.

Carrington, Frank, *Neither Cruel Nor Unusual: The Case for
    Capital Punishment*; New York, Crown, 1978.
Less scholarly than the books by Berns and van den Haag, but
    no less convincing.

——and Lambie, William, *The Defenseless Society*; Ottawa, IL,
    Green Hill, 1976.
Under the force of liberal guilt America has been tying its
    hands and leaving itself defenseless against criminals who
    have never had so much encouragement.

McGuigan, Patrick, and Rader, Randall, eds., *Criminal Justice
    Reform*; Chicago, Regnery/Gateway, 1983.
Like their "judicial reform" volume, this is a blueprint for prac-
    tical conservative action.

Van den Haag, Ernest, *The Death Penalty: A Debate*; New
    York, Plenum Books, 1983.
A vigorous, productive debate; van den Haag, in his best form,
    is pro-capital punishment.

——*Punishing Criminals*; New York, Basic Books, 1975.
Wide-ranging discussion of the nature of punishment, rebutting the idea that it is "revenge" and asserting that adequate punishment is a moral duty of society.

Wilson, James Q., *Thinking About Crime*; New York, Basic Books, 1975.
Wilson, a neoconservative, helped to demolish the liberal myths about crime with this important study; he found that liberals spoke from implicit (and false) premises about human nature, so that his response came to be "as much about how to think about crime (which is to say, how to think about human nature in one of its less attractive forms) as it is about crime itself."

——ed., *Crime and Public Policy*; San Francisco, Institute for Contemporary Studies, 1983.
Hailed as "the most innovative and integrated effort thus far in studying crime," this book's authors propose several fresh policy options, including focusing on incapacitating "career" criminals, lowering the age for compulsory school attendance and lowering minimum wage rates to control youth crime, and encouraging police to use neighborhood "watch" efforts.

——and Richard Herrstein, *Crime and Human Nature*; New York, Simon and Schuster, 1985.
A controversial but heavily researched book arguing that the "criminal personality" is largely influenced by biological factors. Though the debate has raged about the relationship between crime and genetics, this work demonstrates that the liberal belief that environmental factors—chiefly poverty—are responsible for crime is illusory and counter-productive. This is a pioneering study that provides little direct advice on how to change public policy.

Urban Studies

Anderson, Martin, *The Federal Bulldozer*; New York, McGraw-Hill, 1967.
Still the best, most comprehensive condemnation of the federal urban renewal program; Anderson demonstrates that the program produced the opposite effect to that intended, leaving waste and chaos in its wake.

Arkes, Hadley, *The Philosopher in the City: The Moral Dimensions of Urban Politics*; Princeton, Princeton University Press, 1981.
As the title implies, this is a philosophical approach, but one that puts the policy questions into a necessary context.

Banfield, Edward, *The Unheavenly City: The Nature and Future of Our Urban Crisis*; Boston, Little, Brown, 1970.
This blockbuster caused an uproar (mostly among liberals) when it appeared; it argued that the "urban crisis" was in large part a product of utopian expectations and declared that "mammoth government programs" had only "aggravated" serious urban problems.

——*The Unheavenly City Revisited*; Boston, Little, Brown, 1974.
The outcry which followed the publication of *The Unheavenly City* led Banfield to produce this book, which takes up the criticisms of his opponents and furthers his analysis.

Butler, Stuart, *Enterprise Zones: Greenlining the Inner Cities*; New York, Universe Books, 1981.
These zones would significantly reduce the tax and regulatory burden on inner-city businesses in order to stimulate economic growth in blighted areas.

Glazer, Nathan, ed., *Cities in Trouble*; Chicago, Quadrangle, 1970.
Formerly a liberal, now a neoconservative, Glazer came to his new position primarily by seeing the fallacies at the heart of liberal "social planning"; these essays deal with various urban problems.

——and Gorham, William, eds., *The Urban Predicament*; Washington, DC, Urban Institute, 1976.
More of the same.

——and Moynihan, Daniel P., *Beyond the Melting Pot*; Cambridge, MA, MIT Press, 1970.
This study revealed what Michael Novak has called the "unmeltable ethnics"; contrary to abstract liberal notions about "integrating" ethnic groups, Glazer and Moynihan examined the case of New York City and found that it hadn't happened and was not likely to happen within the foreseeable future.

Jacobs, Jane, *The Death & Life of Great American Cities*; New York, Random House, 1961.
Though not a conservative, Jacobs in this book delivered a blistering attack on the mania for urban planning; a book which retains its vitality twenty five years later.

——*The Economy of Cities*; New York, Random House, 1970.
A more focused study, but no less exacting in its strictures against urban utopians.

Social Sciences

Andreski, Stanislav, *Social Sciences As Sorcery*; New York, Penguin, 1974.
British sociologist Andreski lashes out against the fraudulent methodology of the social sciences that turns them from interpretive sciences into the basis for misguided social engineering.

Berger, Peter L., *Introduction to Sociology: A Humanistic Perspective*; New York, Doubleday Anchor, 1963.
In a discipline mired in triviality and ideology, Berger stands out as one of the few men of real stature; this is an excellent introduction to what sociology ought to be.

——*Facing Up to Modernity*; New York, Basic Books, 1977.
Contains some of Berger's best essays, including "The Socialist Myth," "The Greening of American Foreign Policy," and "Intellectual Conservatism: Two Paradoxes."

Machan, Tibor, *The Pseudo-Science of B.F. Skinner*; New Rochelle, NY, Arlington House, 1974.
A telling critique of Skinner's determinism, which may not have much influence in academic circles, but which has filtered down into many popular misconceptions.

Nisbet, Robert, *The Quest for Community*; New York, Oxford University Press, 1953.
Nisbet's classic work argues that the "mediating structures"

that stand between the individual and the state—family, church, union, local region—have been eroded by the expansion of government, thus lessening individual freedom and inducing alienation and insecurity.

——*Social Change and History: Aspects of Western Theory and Development*; New York, Oxford University Press, 1969.
A historical survey of Western concepts of social change from Heraclitus to Talcott Parsons, containing a powerful indictment of the notion of "progress" when applied to a specific political community.

——*The Sociological Tradition*; New York, Basic Books, 1966.
For those who cannot think of sociology without images of the perverse modern ivory tower pseudo-scientists, Nisbet's discussion of the founders and developers of sociology—Tocqueville, Durkheim, Weber—will be a refreshing and informative study.

——*The Twilight of Authority*; New York, Oxford University Press, 1975.
According to Nisbet, the great irony of this century is that as the power of central government has grown, respect for true authority, whether it be religious or political, has waned, leaving a dangerous gap in the psychic well-being of the nation.

Rieff, Philip, *The Triumph of the Therapeutic: Uses of Faith After Freud*; New York, Harper Torchbook, 1968.
With the dissolution of "Christian culture," the emergence of "psychological man" has signaled the triumph of a relativistic ethos which is ultimately a substitute for true spirituality.

Sexuality, the Family and the Social Fabric

Berger, Peter and Neuhaus, Richard John, *To Empower People: The Role of Mediating Structures in Public Policy*; Washington, DC, American Enterprise Institute, 1981.
Mediating structures are those traditional institutions—family, church, union, club—that stand between the individual and the state; under the weight of an interventionist state they have become severely strained, and individual freedom and initiative have been curtailed.

Decter, Midge, *The New Chastity and Other Arguments Against Women's Liberation*; New York, Coward, McCann & Geoghegan, 1972.
Decter's no-nonsense prose has cleared a great deal of fog from the women's lib debate, especially in disentangling the militant ideologues from those guided by common sense.

——*Liberal Parents, Radical Children*; New York, Coward, McCann & Geoghegan, 1975.
. . . as night follows day.

Gilder, George, *Naked Nomads: Unmarried Men in America*; New York, Quadrangle/N.Y. Times Books, 1974.
The percentage of violent crimes committed by unmarried men is staggering; Gilder indicates that public policy which makes marriage unprofitable leads inevitably to murder, rape, and armed robbery.

——*Sexual Suicide*; New York, Quadrangle/N.Y. Times Books, 1973.
This controversial book argued that the violent, short-term impulses of men need to be restrained and rechanneled by the long-term, nurturing aspect of women in the context of marriage; the ironic end of the sexual "liberation" was to reduce women to the short, abusive encounters characteristic of unrestrained masculine behavior.

——*Men and Marriage*; Gretna, LA: Pelican Publishing Co., 1986.
A revised version of *Sexual Suicide,* which it now supersedes.

Howard, John A., ed., *The Family: America's Hope*; Rockford, IL, Rockford Institute, 1979.
Essays by James Hitchcock, Leopold Tyrmand, and others, on this most abused of institutions.

Abortion and Other Life—and Death—Issues

Horan, Dennis J. and Mall, David, eds., *Death, Dying and Euthanasia;* Frederick, MD, University Publications of America, 1982.
Essays concerning an issue which is quickly leaving the theoretical stage and reaching legislative and judicial bodies, especially with regard to so-called "mercy killings."

——and Diamond, Eugene F., eds., *Infanticide and the Handicapped Newborn;* Provo, UT, Brigham Young University Press, 1982.
Another link in the chain, infanticide is a logical outgrowth of the abortion mentality; here too the medical evidence regarding the value of and hope for the handicapped newborn is immense.

Krason, Stephen, *Abortion: Politics, Morality and the Constitution;* Lanham, MD, University Press of America, 1984.
This hefty tome contains a vast amount of legal, medical, philosophical, and constitutional evidence against abortion; at the very least it would make an excellent reference work.

Kreeft, Peter, *The Unaborted Socrates;* Downers Grove, IL, InterVarsity Press, 1983.
Using the Socratic debate format, but with a good dose of healthy laughter, this book cuts to the heart of the matter, and will be especially valuable for young people.

Nathanson, Bernard, *Aborting America*; New York, Doubleday, 1979.
One of the founders of the National Abortion Rights Action League, and a doctor who supervised tens of thousands of abortions, Nathanson came to see abortion as an unmitigated evil; this book tells his story and the reasoning which led him to his about-face.

Noonan, John T., Jr., *A Private Choice*; New York, Free Press, 1979.
Undoubtedly the leading legal authority on the subject of abortion, Noonan here provides the starting point for serious students of the issue.

——ed., *The Morality of Abortion*; Cambridge, MA, Harvard University Press, 1970.
Published before *Roe v. Wade,* this volume nevertheless contains important essays from theological, historical, and political perspectives by John Finnis, John T. Noonan, Jr., Bernard Haring, and others.

Reagan, Ronald, *Abortion and the Conscience of the Nation*; Nashville, TN, Thomas Nelson, 1984.
This urgent plea for life by a sitting president may well become an important historical document when future scholars evaluate the barbarity of our age.

Rice, Charles E., *The Vanishing Right to Live*; Garden City, NY, Doubleday, 1969.
Written by a prominent legal scholar, this 1969 volume is sadly and thoroughly relevant.

Sobran, Joseph, *Single Issues*; New York, Human Life Press, 1983.
Columnist and *National Review* Senior Editor, Sobran tackles such single issues as abortion, euthanasia, and homosexuality with a calm but strictly reasoned approach.

Faith & Freedom: Conservatives on Religion

Atkins, Stanley, and Theodore McConnell, eds., *Churches on the Wrong Road*; Chicago, Regnery Gateway, 1986.
Essays on the politicization of Christianity by Gerhart Niemeyer, Russell Kirk, and James V. Schall, among others.

Berger, Peter, *A Rumor of Angels*; Garden City, NY, Doubleday, 1970.
Argues against the "alleged demise" of the supernatural and outlines the sociological insights which can support religion.

——*The Sacred Canopy: Elements of a Sociological Theory of Religion*; Garden City, NY, Doubleday, 1967.
The "sociology of knowledge" is used to shed light on the contemporary religious situation.

Blamires, Harry, *The Christian Mind*; Ann Arbor, MI, Servant Press, 1978.
Christians have allowed their own thinking to be taken over by secular categories; they must return to an awareness of evil, dogma, and sacramental reality.

Brown, Harold O.J., *Heresies: The Image of Christ in the Mirror of Heresy and Orthodoxy from the Apostles to the Present*; Garden City, NY, Doubleday, 1984.
Brown is a Protestant theologian who has long registered his dissent with doctrinal and political liberalism in the

mainstream churches; here he provides a useful historical survey of those who take only part of the truth for the whole.

Eliot, T.S., *Christianity and Culture*; New York, Harcourt, Brace & World, 1968.
This volume comprises *The Idea of a Christian Society* and *Notes Towards the Definition of Culture*. In both Eliot declares that liberalism, a "loosening" of morality and belief in the supernatural, leads inevitably to paganism and tyranny; only orthodox Christianity can bind men in community and nourish culture.

Herberg, Will, *Protestant Catholic Jew*; Garden City, NY, Doubleday Anchor, 1960.
Widely considered the finest sociological study of American religion; written by a conservative scholar with no axes to grind.

Hitchcock, James, *Catholicism and Modernity*; New York, Seabury Press, 1979.
Of interest to Catholics and non-Catholics alike; the effects of secularism, including "therapeutic" psychology, and the growth of a "New Class" church bureaucracy, are meticulously documented and analyzed.

——*What Is Secular Humanism?*; Ann Arbor, MI, Servant Press, 1982.
Simple, readable explanation of a phenomenon that is too often reduced to a mere epithet.

Howard, John A., ed., *Belief, Faith & Reason*; Belfast, Christian Journals Limited, 1981.
Essays by such writers as Stanley Jaki, Edmund Fuller, and Stephen Tonsor touching on the relationship between religion and law, science, and politics.

Howard, Thomas, *Chance or the Dance? A Critique of Modern Secularism*; Wheaton, IL, Harold Shaw, 1979.
Beautifully written attack on the "New Myth" of secular scientism, which has supplanted the "Old Myth" of religion.

Jaki, Stanley L., *Cosmos and Creator*; Chicago, Regnery/ Gateway, 1982.
Using the latest cosmological discoveries and theories, Jaki shows that science, contrary to the propaganda of various positivists, provides information which is completely consonant with religious belief in a Creator.

Kilpatrick, William K., *Psychological Seduction: The Failure of Modern Psychology*; Nashville, TN, Thomas Nelson, 1983.
A penetrating revelation of how Christians themselves have come to equate "self-esteem" and "personal growth" with salvation; in short, Original Sin and "I'm OK, You're OK" don't mix.

Lawler, Philip F., *The Ultimate Weapon*; Chicago, Regnery/ Gateway, 1984.
A prudent and well-reasoned response to the American bishops' pastoral on nuclear arms, upholding the morality of deterrence in the context of just war theory, and concluding that the ultimate weapon against oppression is . . . prayer.

Lefever, Ernest W., *Amsterdam to Nairobi: The World Council of Churches and the Third World*; Washington, DC, Ethics and Public Policy Center, 1979.
Looking beneath the rhetoric of Christian "compassion," Lefever finds that the WCC has become dominated by ideologues whose crusades have aided Marxist revolutionaries who are far from championing the poor and downtrodden.

Lewis, C.S., *The Abolition of Man*; New York, Macmillan, 1965.
Classic and prophetic demonstration that a rejection of natural law leads to totalitarianism; "man's conquest of nature" really means some men conquering others through the use of science.

——*Mere Christianity*; New York, Macmillan, 1960.
Perhaps the greatest work of Christian apologetics in this century; Lewis upholds the central doctrines of the Faith against modernists who would reduce Christ to a "great moral teacher." Also contains a trenchant defense of Christian morality.

——*God in the Dock: Essays on Theology and Ethics*; Grand Rapids, MI, 1970.
Many outstanding essays on such topics as "Religion Without Dogma?", "The Humanitarian Theory of Punishment," and "Must Our Image of God Go?"

Muggeridge, Malcolm, *Jesus Rediscovered*; Garden City, NY, Doubleday, 1969.
This is the book in which the brilliant, iconoclastic, and cynical British journalist came to admit that there was a spiritual reality to which we must all awaken; his talents baptized, Muggeridge uses them to dissect the follies of a secular, hedonistic age.

——*Christ and the Media*; Grand Rapids, MI, Wm. B. Eerdmans, 1977.
Speaking from long experience as a media man, Muggeridge relentlessly uncovers the inherent element of "fantasy" in television, opposing to it the objective truth of Christianity.

Murray, John Courtney, S.J., *We Hold These Truths*; New York, Doubleday Image, 1964.

An important work claiming that the American political tradition is consistent with the Catholic understanding of natural law and rejecting the idea of America as a creation of modern "natural rights" theory; the basic thrust of this book should be of interest to all conservatives, Catholic or not.

Nash, Ronald H., *Social Justice and the Christian Church*; Milford, MI, Mott Media, 1983.
Nash, a Protestant theologian and philosopher, makes clear the difference between compassion and utopianism.

———ed., *Liberation Theology*; Milford, MI, Mott Media, 1984.
Essays by Michael Novak, Carl Henry, Richard Neuhaus, and others criticizing the reduction of religion to radical politics in this latest theological heresy.

Neuhaus, Richard John, *The Naked Public Square: Religion and Democracy in America*; Grand Rapids, MI, Eerdmans, 1984.
Lutheran theologian and former radical, Pastor Neuhaus says that religion should have a public role, but that it must speak to the moral issues essential to its nature instead of adopting secular standards.

Niebuhr, H. Richard, *Christ and Culture*; New York, Harper Colophon, 1975.
A profound meditation on the way Christianity not only informs culture but criticizes it as well.

Novak, Michael, *Freedom with Justice: Catholic Social Thought and Liberal Institutions*; San Francisco, Harper & Row, 1984.
Novak differs from the conventional wisdom that interprets papal social doctrine as being socialistic; he examines the history of classical liberalism and concludes that the Church's teaching can be consistent with a free economy.

——*The Spirit of Democratic Capitalism*; New York, Simon & Schuster, 1982.
Without the mystical language of George Gilder, Novak emphasizes the spiritual dimension to a risk- and sacrifice-making market economy.

Reichley, A. James, *Religion in American Public Life*; Washington, DC: Brookings Institution, 1985.
That the publisher of this book is the traditionally liberal Brookings Institution is extremely significant, for as Joseph Sobran has written, Reichley "confirms nearly every conservative thesis about the role of religion in our politics and history." The historical and topical conclusions presented here argue against the liberal misinterpretation of the First Amendment and the "watertight" theory of the separation of church and state.

Rice, Charles E., *Beyond Abortion: The Theory and Practice of the Secular State*; Chicago, Franciscan Herald Press, 1978.
A frightening but all-too-plausible argument that Americans will be left with no constitutional grounds with which to defend religious beliefs and traditional morality.

Schall, James V., S.J., *Liberation Theology*; San Francisco, Ignatius Press, 1982.
Drawing on a wide knowledge of theology and political science, Schall demolishes the fundamental ideas behind liberationism.

——*The Politics of Heaven and Hell*; Lanham, MD, University Press of America, 1984.
An excellent sourcebook for an understanding of the relation between politics and theology.

——ed., *Out of Justice, Peace and Winning the Peace*; San Francisco, Ignatius Press, 1984.

Almost unreported in America were the bishops' pastorals in France and Germany on the subject of war and peace (reprinted here), both of which roundly affirmed the morality of deterrence and American strength.

Stanmeyer, William, *Clear & Present Danger*; Ann Arbor, MI, Servant Press, 1983.
A legal scholar delves into the tortuous and confused decisions by various courts on the relationship between church and state, noting the dangers and pointing out the road back to sanity.

Vitz, Paul C., *Psychology as Religion: The Cult of Self Worship*; Grand Rapids, MI, Eerdmans, 1977.
This is the best analysis of how psychology has substituted itself for religion.

Race, Minorities and Quota Hiring

Capaldi, Nicholas, *Out of Order: Affirmative Action and the Crisis of Doctrinaire Liberalism*; Buffalo: Prometheus Books, 1985.
A major critique of affirmative action, with special reference to its role in destroying higher education in America.

Eastland, Terry and Bennett, William J., *Counting by Race: Equality from the Founding Fathers to Bakke*; New York, Basic Books, 1979.
Hard-hitting, persuasive study which moves beyond the rhetoric of "rights" to examine the flimsy, if not non-existent, case for quotas in the American political tradition.

Gilder, George, *Visible Man: A True Story of Post-Racist America*; New York, Basic Books, 1978.
A moving, vivid piece of social observation; Gilder writes: "The real meaning of the young black criminal, who struts in the spotlights of the media and the university, eludes nearly all who study him. . . . Belittled by pity and charity and sociology, he becomes less a man than a confluence of social pressures. He is said to be crippled by racism. . . brutalized by bigoted cops, a victim of 'bad' schools and 'bad' housing. He becomes a specter of forces. . . but scarcely a person himself."

Glazer, Nathan, *Affirmative Discrimination: Ethnic Inequality and Public Policy*; New York, Basic Books, 1978.

The essence of American politics since the Founding has been the primacy of the individual; but, according to Glazer, the policy of "affirmative action" actually causes injustice to, and restricts the freedom of, individuals by raising social "groups" to a dominant role in society.

Moynihan, Daniel P., *Maximum Feasible Misunderstanding*; New York, Free Press, 1969.
See under "The Welfare State."

Murray, Charles, *Losing Ground: American Social Policy, 1950-1980*; New York, Basic Books, 1984.
See under "The Welfare State."

Novak, Michael and Rossi, Peter, eds., *The Rise of the Unmeltable Ethnics*; New York, Macmillan, 1971.
Despite the evidence, the liberal myth of uniformitarianism persists; these essays attempt to understand and promote the value of ethnic groupings in America.

Roche, George C., *The Balancing Act: Quota Hiring in Higher Education*; La Salle, IL, Open Court, 1974.
Roche argues that "affirmative action" programs, in addition to their inherent injustice, threaten the whole notion of standards of excellence in education.

Sowell, Thomas, *Affirmative Action: Was it Necessary in Academia?*; Washington, DC, American Enterprise Institute, 1975.
Sowell's answer is no; his own achievement is eloquent testimony to that belief.

——*Civil Rights: Rhetoric or Reality?*; New York, Wm. Morrow, 1984.
A tough, polemical approach to an emotionally-charged issue; Sowell says that many of the civil rights pressure groups

are not satisfied with equal opportunity but pursue an egalitarian program, ignoring the rule of law and the Western tradition of individual freedom.

——*Ethnic America: A History*; New York, Basic Books, 1981.
Synthesizing and ordering a massive amount of research, Sowell examines the many immigrants to America, noting what characteristics led them to their economic and political positions in society; his findings are often surprising and contrary to traditional stereotypes; *The New York Times* said this was a "quiet but powerful attack on liberal beliefs about minorities, racism, segregation and affirmative action."

——*Markets and Minorities*; New York, Basic Books, 1981.
See under "The Welfare State."

——*Race and Economics*; New York, D. McKay, 1975.
See under "The Welfare State."

Williams, Walter E., *America: A Minority Viewpoint*; Stanford, CA, Hoover Institution Press, 1982.
"Individual freedom is and always has been a radical idea. It was radical in 1775 and it is radical today"; in the 84 newspaper columns collected here, Williams advocates the moral and economic superiority of the free market, and affirmative action and other "pro-minority" policies come under his relentless analysis.

——*The State Against Blacks*; New York, New Press, 1982.
See under "The Welfare State."

——*Youth and Minority Unemployment*; Stanford, CA, Hoover Institution Press, 1977.
Among the other issues discussed in this book is one of the finest cases against the minimum wage laws ever written.

Wortham, Anne, *The Other Side of Racism: A Philosophical Study of Black Race Consciousness*; Columbus, OH, Ohio State University Press, 1981.

Though the civil rights movement had legitimate ends, certain elements within it were motivated by only marginally related interests, and instead launched an effort to institute reverse discrimination and radical egalitarianism.

The Media

Bethell, Tom, *Television Evening News Covers Inflation: 1978-79*; Washington, DC, Media Institute, 1980.

Belittled as secondary to "unemployment," inflation has often been treated as a mystery, rather than a direct result of a government living beyond its means; Bethell's analysis uncovers many of the mystifying clichés of liberalism.

Braestrup, Peter, *Big Story: How the American Press & Television Reported & Interpreted the Crises of Tet 1968 in Vietnam & Washington,* 2 vols.; Boulder, CO, Westview Press, 1977.

Braestrup's voluminous research led him to a simple, but terrifying conclusion: the media coverage of the Tet Offensive made the situation out to be much more of a "defeat" than it actually was; the negative reaction to this campaign in turn led to a significant shift in opinion in which, for the first time, a majority was against the war.

Braley, Russell, *Bad News: The Foreign Policy of the New York Times;* Chicago, Regnery/Gateway, 1984.

Braley, a veteran journalist, has compiled a thorough, readable account of the leftist bias of the foreign policy news in the *Times,* which has in many instances influenced the course of events, as in the case where a *Times* correspondent turned Fidel Castro from a provincial rebel leader into a superstar overnight.

Efron, Edith, *The News Twisters*; Los Angeles, Nash Publishing, 1971.

A milestone in the conservative critique of the media, this controversial best-seller, made up of statistical analysis of national television news coverage of the presidential candidates in the 1968 election, demonstrated the anti-Nixon, pro-liberal bias of the three networks.

———and Chambers, Clytia, *How CBS Tried to Kill a Book*; Los Angeles, Nash Publishing, 1972.

The book was *The News Twisters.*

Kowet, Don, *A Matter of Honor: General William C. Westmoreland versus CBS*; New York, MacMillan, 1984.

The case ended in a stalemate that was generally perceived to be a victory for CBS, but this book, which preceded the case, contains much of the incriminating evidence against the ideologues who produced the CBS documentary on the casualty counts during the Vietnam War.

Lawler, Philip F., *The Alternative Influence: The Impact of Investigative Reporting on America's Media*; Washington, DC, Media Institute, 1984.

"Investigative" and "adversarial" reporting are terms that often serve as convenient cloaks to hide an ideological agenda and methods of an ethically questionable nature.

Phillips, Kevin P., *Mediacracy: American Parties and Politics in the Communications Age*; New York, Doubleday, 1975.

"Mediacracy" translates as "rule by the media," but it also sounds suspiciously like "mediocrity"; Phillips explores the implications of both in this energetically argued book.

Rothman, Stanley and Lichter, S. Robert, *The Media Elite and*

American Values; Washington, DC, Ethics and Public Policy Center, 1982; reprinted from *Public Opinion,* October/November 1981.

The result of a massive questionnaire/survey project, this study concludes that the media elite are largely upper-middle-class, East coast professionals who are ideologically liberal—a surprise to no one, but here scientifically documented.

Theberge, Leonard J., ed., *TV Coverage of the Oil Crises: How Well Was the Public Served?*; New York, Pergamon, 1982.

Given that the economics of federal regulation of the oil business was rarely mentioned, and that the oil companies were made to serve as scapegoats for the "crisis," the public was ill-served indeed.

——ed., *Crooks, Conmen and Clowns: Businessmen in TV Entertainment*; Washington, DC, Media Institute, 1981.

How seriously the public takes the ruthless, cigar-chomping businessmen of TV shows, those corporate moguls who so conveniently embody all evil, is uncertain; but the bias is there, and is evaluated in this series of essays.

Wattenberg, Ben, *The Good News is the Bad News is Wrong*; New York, Simon & Schuster, 1984.

According to one reviewer, this book "rebuts the professional pessimists—the experts, observers, and pundits who make it sound as if 'we are living in a desperate moment' "; Wattenberg goes on to supply the unnewsworthy reports about increasing prosperity, important medical gains, and the like.

History: Some Conservative Revisionism

Berthoff, Rowland, *An Unsettled People: Social Order and Disorder in American History*; New York, Harper & Row, 1971.
Russell Kirk has called this book "a remarkably perceptive examination of the tension of order and freedom, by a conservatively inclined historian."

Buckley, William F., and Bozell, L. Brent, *McCarthy and His Enemies*; New Rochelle, NY, Arlington House, 1983.
The dust storm that was whipped up by anti-McCarthy hysteria has now settled into a hard crust of self-righteous myth; the calm message of this volume is that despite his failings, McCarthy was right about Communist subversion in government and that his efforts were often frustrated or ignored by his congressional colleagues.

Chamberlain, John, *The Enterprising Americans: A Business History of the United States*; New York, Harper & Row, 1963.
See under "Economics."

Gottfried, Paul, *Conservative Millenarians: The Romantic Experience in Bavaria*; New York, Fordham University Press, 1979.
The conservative romantics who are the subject of this book are not well known among contemporary conservatives, but there is much to learn from this group, who strove for

spiritual and political order in a time of ideology and centralization.

Handlin, Oscar, *The Distortion of America*; Boston, Little, Brown, 1981.
A leading historian speaks out against the leftist denigration of American institutions which has demoralized us at home, and paralyzed our policy abroad.

——*Truth in History*; Cambridge, MA, Harvard University Press, 1979.
The gaggle of ideologies now prominent in the field of history, including Marxism, feminism, and "psycho-history," call into question the idea of historical truth; Handlin addresses the issues in a prudent, thoughtful manner.

Hayek, Friedrich von, ed., *Capitalism and the Historians*; Chicago, University of Chicago Press, 1963.
In the textbooks and even the scholarly literature, the period of the Industrial Revolution has been almost uniformly considered to consist of merciless capitalists grinding the poor to early deaths; the reality was more complex, and the essays gathered here help to set the record straight.

Himmelfarb, Gertrude, *The Idea of Poverty: England in the Early Industrial Age*; New York, Knopf, 1984.
"History is full of discrepancies between what historians believe to be fact and what contemporaries thought to be such"; Himmelfarb's survey of ideas about poverty in both the politics and the literature of the Industrial Revolution is a model of balance and restraint.

Jaki, Stanley L., *The Road of Science and the Ways to God*; Chicago, University of Chicago Press, 1978.
The Carl Sagan view of scientific history is that the bright promise of the Greeks was shattered by the superstitious know-nothingism of Christianity, only to be recovered by

the secular Renaissance; Jaki demolishes this scheme in his Gifford Lectures by showing that the Christian belief in an objective, ordered universe (especially during the Middle Ages) was the basis for modern scientific progress.

——*The Origin of Science and the Science of its Origin*; Chicago, Regnery/Gateway, 1978.
A shorter book than the one cited above, it focuses in on the medieval worldview that led to the rise of modern science; dominated as the history of science is by secular positivism, this and other works by Jaki are indispensable.

Johnson, Paul, *Modern Times: The World from the Twenties to the Eighties*; New York, Harper & Row, 1983.
Only a writer of Johnson's encyclopedic knowledge and masterful style could have produced this survey, which is dominated by the recurring theme of the growth of ideological states; Johnson writes: "Throughout these years, the power of the State to do evil expanded with awesome speed. Its power to do good grew slowly and ambiguously."

Kraditor, Aileen S., *The Radical Persuasion, 1890-1917*; Baton Rouge, LA, Louisiana State University Press, 1981.
The subject of this study is the radical political movements at the turn of the century, but it also illuminates many of the issues pertinent to social and labor history.

Lewy, Guenter, *America in Vietnam*; New York, Oxford University Press, 1978.
Norman Podhoretz has called Lewy's volume "authoritative"; it is easily the best, ideology-free history of the Vietnam War.

Lukacs, John, *A History of the Cold War*; Garden City, NY, Doubleday Anchor, 1966.

Lukacs argues that the division between American and Russian spheres of interest as they have developed since the eighteenth century is "the supreme condition of contemporary history. . . not the Atomic Bomb and not Communism."

——*Historical Consciousness, or the Remembered Past*; New York, Schocken Books, 1985.
A path-breaking work which contends that historical consciousness has become a new mode of thought, one that can help us to transcend the pride and madness of a present-centered culture.

——*The Passing of the Modern Age*; New York, Harper Torchbooks, 1970.
The striking and provocative thesis of this book is difficult to summarize; it maintains that the modern age, 1500-19—, is dissolving (the essays proving this are the heart of the book); Lukacs is unsure whether a dark age or a renaissance will follow.

——*The Last European War: September 1939-December 1941*; New York, Doubleday Anchor, 1976.
One of the most important studies of twentieth century European history; Lukacs holds that after 1941 Russia and America became the dominant actors on the world stage.

——*Outgrowing Democracy: A History of the United States in the Twentieth Century*; New York, Doubleday, 1984.
Peppered with Lukacs's controversial pronouncements, this cultural and political survey examines the ironic fact that as America reached its greatest power in the world, it was at the same time declining internally.

Lynn, Kenneth S., *The Air-Line to Seattle*; Chicago, University of Chicago Press, 1983.

Witty, urbane, and angry, these essays on historical and literary subjects from Emerson to Hemingway assail the tendency of intellectuals to superimpose their ideological formulas on their material.

Maddox, Robert James, *The New Left and the Origins of the Cold War*; Princeton, Princeton University Press, 1973.
Taking the books of seven leading "revisionist" historians of the New Left, Maddox proves that they have deliberately falsified the historical record; as he puts it, "a growing body of academic historians consistently misuses the fundamental sources of a crucial era in American history."

McDonald, Forrest, *A Constitutional History of the United States*; New York, Franklin Watts, 1982.
Though written as an undergraduate textbook, it is a thoroughly readable history written from a conservative stance, one that resolutely denies that the written Constitution can be ignored in favor of the ideological preferences of individual justices.

——*Alexander Hamilton: A Biography*; New York, W.W. Norton, 1979.
Hamilton has had countless detractors, and his vision of a commercial republic has not satisfied all conservatives, but he receives here a vigorous, well-written, sympathetic treatment.

——*We the People: The Economic Origins of the Constitution*; Chicago, University of Chicago Press, 1958.
McDonald, in a feat of brilliant and impassioned scholarship, almost singlehandedly dismantled the "economic" interpretation of the Constitution put forward by the immensely influential historian, Charles Beard, and opened the way to a recovery of the statesmanship of the Founding Fathers.

———*E Pluribus Unum: The Formation of the American Republic*; Indianapolis, Liberty Press, 1979.
McDonald claimed that *We the People* was intended to "clear the decks" of the myths about the Constitution; this is the study of the Founding made possible by that earlier book.

———*Novus Ordo Seclorum: The Intellectual Origins of the Constitution*; Lawrence, KS: University Press of Kansas, 1985.
The final volume of the trilogy beginning with *We the People* and *E Pluribus Unum*; moving from the interplay between economics and politics which was the subject of the second volume, McDonald here surveys the intellectual background to the Constitution.

McWhiney, Grady, *Southerners and Other Americans*; New York, Basic Books, 1964.
A leading Southern historian here provides a healthily different perspective to that of the century of ingrained Yankee snobbery that permeates the prevailing "wisdom."

Morgan, H. Wayne, ed., *The Gilded Age: A Reappraisal*; Syracuse, NY, Syracuse University Press, 1963.
Though not a conservative himself, Morgan has put together a significant work of revisionism about a period in American history too easily caricatured.

Nash, George, *The Life of Herbert Hoover; Volume I, The Engineer, 1874-1914*; New York, W.W. Norton, 1984.
Hoover may not have taken consistently conservative actions while President, but he is a complex figure who has been sniffed at by FDR-adoring historians; this first of several volumes covers Hoover the entrepreneur.

Nock, Albert Jay, *Jefferson*; New York, Hill & Wang, 1960.

Nock said of this work that it is not a biography but "a study in conduct and character"; for Nock it is Jefferson the thinker rather than Jefferson the political actor that matters, and he produced a searching, if somewhat eccentric, exploration of that most complex of presidents.

Podhoretz, Norman, *Why We Were in Vietnam*; New York, Simon & Schuster, 1982.

America may have been reckless in entering the Vietnam War, but it was not immoral or criminal; Podhoretz not only examines why we went in and stayed in, but also produces a penetrating critique of those who claimed that the war was a completely evil thing.

Radosh, Ronald, and Milton, Joyce, *The Rosenberg File*; New York, Holt, Rinehart & Winston, 1983.

Like Allen Weinstein in his study of the Hiss-Chambers case, the authors started out believing in the innocence of the Rosenbergs, but an exhaustive research process into both old and new sources convinced them that the truth was otherwise.

Russell, Francis, *Sacco & Vanzetti: The Case Resolved*; New York: Harper & Row, 1986.

Russell published *Tragedy in Dedham,* on the Sacco and Vanzetti case, in 1962, concluding that Sacco was guilty of murder and that Vanzetti was not; this book, based on access to FBI files, "resolves" the case beyond question. More importantly, it debunks most of the myths about these martyrs of the Left and thus is a major study in ideological history and distortion.

Scott, Otto J., *The Secret Six: John Brown and the Abolitionist Movement*; New York, Times Books, 1979.

Scott's study of these abolitionists has a strikingly contemporary significance, for he demonstrates that they were among the first of a peculiarly modern breed: ideological terrorists.

Shapiro, Edward S., *Clio from the Right: Essays of a Conservative Historian*; Lanham, MD, University Press of America, 1983.
The essays collected here deal with several major subjects, including Southern history, the iconology of liberalism, the Cold War, and Jewish political and social concerns.

Silver, Thomas, *Coolidge and the Historians*; Durham, SC, Carolina Academic Press, 1982.
Rather than a study of Coolidge, this book is more of an attack on the tendentious, myth-making scholarship of historians like Arthur Schlesinger, Jr. who have obscured the Coolidge era.

Sumner, William Graham, *The Conquest of the United States By Spain and Other Essays*; 1905; reprinted, Chicago, Henry Regnery.
Sumner was among the few who did not join the imperialist fever of the Spanish-American war, and his early revisionism on this period retains all its tough ironic insight.

Ulam, Adam, *A History of Soviet Russia*; New York, Holt, Rinehart & Winston, 1976.
Given the difficulties of the subject, Ulam's books on Soviet history are a testament to rigorous scholarship and honesty.

Weinstein, Allan, *Perjury: The Hiss-Chambers Trial*; New York, Random House, 1978.
Weinstein became something of a neoconservative in the process of writing this study, which began as an attempt to prove Hiss innocent; Weinstein's conclusion is that the verdict stands.

Education

Babbitt, Irving, *Literature and the American College*; Clifton, NJ, Augustus Kelly, 1972.
Babbitt's contention is that the imagination can be demonic or idyllic as well as moral, and that this distinction has been blurred in the academic realm.

Barzun, Jacques, *The House of Intellect*; New York, Harper & Row, 1959.
The conservative criticism contained in this book, Barzun says, applies to "any nation that adopts egalitarian democracy, mass education and journalism, the cult of art and philanthropy, and the manners coincident with these."

——*Teacher in America*; Indianapolis, IN, Liberty Press, 1981.
Barzun believes that education cannot be neatly prearranged, that the teacher must suggest the complexity and depth of his material, and that teaching "method" is less important than the teacher's absorption in the subject itself.

Blumenfeld, Samuel, *N.E.A.: Trojan Horse in American Education*; Boise, ID, Paradigm, 1984.
The NEA began as a professional association but has become a union and the most powerful lobby in Washington; Blumenfeld traces the NEA's radical stands on "values clarification," sex education, and its increasing intolerance of private schools, discipline, and rigorous education.

Buckley, William F., *God and Man at Yale*; Chicago, Regnery/ Gateway, 1977.
See under "The Conservative as Witness: Personal Testimony."

Bunzel, John H., ed., *Challenge to American Schools: The Case for Standards and Values*; New York, Oxford University Press, 1985.
The contributors to this volume (including Brigitte Berger, Nathan Glazer, and Diane Ravitch) dismantle most of the liberal myths about education, examining such areas as curriculum, teachers unions, and the role of judicial activism in education.

Burleigh, Anne Husted, ed., *Education in a Free Society*; Indianapolis, IN, Liberty Press, 1973.
Essays by Russell Kirk, Stephen Tonsor, Henry Manne, and Gottfried Dietze, plus Dorothy Sayers's famous essay, "The Lost Tools of Learning."

Chalmers, Gordon Keith, *The Republic and the Person*; Chicago, Henry Regnery, 1952.
Douglas Bush wrote of this work that education has been "corrupted by 'disintegrated liberalism,' by damp humanitarianism and dry instrumentalism. . . . Instead of the social conditioning and teaching by generalities, the inculcation of 'attitudes,' Dr. Chambers would revive a much older. . .concept of liberal education. . .based on the moral verities of human experience, one that demands both solid knowledge and rational activity."

Ericson, Edward E., *Radicals in the University*; Stanford, CA, Hoover Institution Press, 1975.
Ericson writes not so much about the student movement as the young faculty members who joined the New Left organizations, Students for a Democratic Society and the New University Conference; he concludes that the polarity be-

tween the "personal" and the "political" made by the radicals led them to eventual frustration and dissolution.

Everhart, Robert B., *The Public School Monopoly: A Critical Analysis of Education and the State in American Society*; San Francisco, Pacific Institute, 1984.
The essays in this collection come from members of both left and right, and include historical background, a critique of the way state regulation of education actually works against minorities and the disadvantaged, and policy alternatives such as vouchers, private schools, and tuition tax credits.

Glazer, Nathan, ed., *Bureaucrats and Brainpower: Government Regulation of Universities*; San Francisco, Institute for Contemporary Studies, 1979.
Since the federal government has been increasingly holding the pursestrings in higher education, it has acted as a conduit for a radical impulse which has sought to restructure the universities on an ideological pattern; the essays here treat the effects of government intervention and suggest a way out.

Hart, Benjamin, *Poisoned Ivy*; New York, Stein & Day, 1984.
The founder of the controversial *Dartmouth Review* writes of God and man at his alma mater, which is dominated by a sanctimonious and mindless liberalism.

Kirk, Russell, *Decadence and Renewal in the Higher Learning*; Chicago, Regnery/Gateway, 1978.
This is Kirk's *magnum opus* on education, encompassing thirty years' worth of study and criticism; in fact, the book is arranged chronologically, and Kirk takes up the various themes that have arisen over time.

——*Academic Freedom*; Chicago, Henry Regnery, 1955.

Like so many liberal god-words, anything can be perpetrated in the name of "academic freedom," including the most perverse and radical activities; when the cult of "academic freedom" first began to be felt, Kirk wrote what may still be the best book on the subject.

Ladd, Everett Carll, Jr., and Lipset, Seymour Martin, *The Divided Academy: Professors & Politics*; New York, McGraw-Hill, 1975.
Examining the data gathered by two major surveys of the academic community revealed that professors are indeed predominantly "liberal-left."

Lawler, Philip F., *Coughing in Ink*; Lanham, MD, University Press of America, 1983.
A wide-ranging critique of college education at present, arguing that the pursuit of truth has been replaced by utilitarianism and ideology; Lawler suggests several interesting ways of bringing about change, including more assertive trustees.

Martin, William Oliver, *Order and Integration of Knowledge*; Ann Arbor, MI, University of Michigan Press, 1957.
"Subjectivism, and intellectual, moral, and spiritual nihilism are no longer the bookish theories of men of pride—they have become a part of our culture. . . . The tragedy of our age is the awful incommunicability of souls." Martin's philosophical study is an attempt to undo the effects of over-specialization and decadence.

Nisbet, Robert, *The Degradation of the Academic Dogma: The University in America, 1945-1970*; New York, Basic Books, 1971.
A leading conservative sociologist takes aim at the triviality and trendiness that have hampered the traditional mission of higher education.

Phenix, Philip, *Education and the Common Good: A Moral Philosophy of the Curriculum*; New York, Harper & Row, 1961.

A call for the re-investment of moral and spiritual values in the curriculum; the book's central theme is the distinction between the "life of desire," or self-satisfaction, and the "life of worth," which involves intelligence, creativity, conscience, and reverence.

Powers, Richard, *The Dilemma of Education in a Democracy*; Chicago, Regnery/Gateway, 1984.

"The most despicable villains" in the failure of our educational system "have been our professional educators, for among the guilty only they may be said to be profiteers. Not that they have been the source of our ills. . . . They offer easy remedies to ills which seem to be incurable by rational means, or curable only at a price which cannot or will not be paid."

Ravitch, Diane, *The Troubled Crusade: American Education, 1945-1980*; New York, Basic Books, 1983.

Ravitch is not a conservative, but she is honest enough to have provided a history of education that does not shirk the obvious, such as the liberal attempt to make education directly solve all social ills, an effort which ended in poor education and worsened social pathology.

Roche, George, *Education in America*; Hillsdale, MI, Hillsdale College Press, 1969.

The president of Hillsdale College outlines what a truly liberal education should be.

——*The Balancing Act: Quota Hiring in Higher Education*; La Salle, IL, Open Court, 1974.

See under "Race, Minorities, and Quota Hiring."

Sowell, Thomas, *Black Education: Myths and Tragedies*; New York, D. McKay, 1972.

Sowell shows that the "myths" are responsible in large part for the "tragedies" of black education; the well-intentioned humanitarian efforts to help blacks have often been patronizing and counter-productive.

——*Education: Assumptions Versus History*; Stanford, CA: Hoover Institution Press, 1986.

Various essays by Sowell are brought together here: they cover the controversies over affirmative action, race and IQ, tuition tax credits, and academic tenure.

Tonsor, Stephen, *Tradition and Reform in Education*; La Salle, IL, Open Court, 1974.

Among Tonsor's conclusions: the role of government in education should be limited to modest financial support and the maintenance of standards and accreditation; values and authority should be returned to academia, and private and church-related colleges must reclaim the identity they lost in trying to imitate state universities.

Literature and Cultural Criticism

Bellow, Saul, *The Dean's December;* New York, Harper & Row, 1982.

Bellow has been called an "intellectual" novelist, and many of his fictions concern some aspect of American politics, culture, and art; throughout his career he has resolutely cut across the liberal grain, and this latest novel finds him exploring the contrasts and similitudes between East and West.

Berman, Ronald, *Culture and Politics;* Lanham, MD, University Press of America, 1984.

A literary critic and former director of the National Endowment for the Arts, Berman attacks the politicization of the grant-making process.

Bradbury, Ray, *Dandelion Wine;* New York, Bantam, 1969.

Russell Kirk has praised Bradbury's "moral imagination," which has employed the science fiction form to explore enduring themes such as man's fallen nature.

Brooks, Cleanth, *The Well Wrought Urn;* New York, Harcourt Brace Jovanovich, 1956.

The distinguished Southern critic, an associate of Robert Penn Warren and others of the Southern Agrarian school, has always shown a deep appreciation of the "permanent things," as in his magisterial works on William Faulkner; this volume is a classic of modern literary criticism.

Cather, Willa, *Death Comes for the Archbishop;* New York, Random House, 1971.

It has become fashionable to concentrate on Cather's professional, social, and hypothetical sex life, all supposedly indicating a "liberal" sensibility, but such readings are impositions on the traditional vision of her art, which was nurtured on the Great Plains in her youth.

De Vries, Peter, *I Hear America Swinging;* Boston, Little, Brown, 1976.

George Will is an avid proponent of this unjustly neglected comic novelist who satirizes the upper middle class, East coast society so dominant in business, government, and academia.

Dos Passos, John, *District of Columbia,* a trilogy comprising *Adventures of a Young Man, Number One,* and *The Grand Design;* Boston, Houghton Mifflin, 1952.

His early novels are full of social protest against business bosses oppressing workers, but his increasing conservatism led him later to protest the union bosses; an overarching consistency in his art is a rejection of the collective use of power to stifle individuality and human dignity.

Eliot, T.S., *Selected Essays, 1917-1932;* New York, Harcourt, Brace, 1932.

Like the other great modernist writers, Ezra Pound and James Joyce, Eliot was deeply committed to preserving the symbols and literature of the West by "making them new"; his critical essays, masterpieces of non-specialist writing, did just that.

Frost, Robert, *Poetry & Prose;* New York, Holt, Rinehart & Winston, 1973.

Frost never fit into the liberal categories for a true artist: he was not an alienated, rootless, chaotic personality, but a New Englander, and a traditionalist with a finely tuned moral sensibility.

Griffin, Bryan, *Panic of the Philistines;* Chicago, Regnery/ Gateway, 1983.
Griffin's tragicomic attack on the vulgarity, mediocrity, and smugness of the literary establishment drew this response from a critic: "Singularly irritating. . . yet many of the writers he holds up to ridicule have asked for it. . . He sees that many of our literary emperors have no clothes on, and he's willing to say so. . . ."

Hawthorne, Nathaniel, *The Blithedale Romance;* New York, W.W. Norton, 1977.
Hawthorne's brooding awareness of man's darker side prevented him from embracing a bland optimism about the inevitability of progress; in this novel he subjects one utopian community of his time, the Transcendentalist Brook Farm, to a powerful moral searchlight, and finds it wanting.

James, Henry, *The Bostonians;* New York, New American Library, 1980.
Though political terms cannot be applied to James, his acute observation of the social scene allowed him to evoke the larger themes that lie behind particular events; this novel exposes the flaws in radical feminism without wholly endorsing the "traditional" way of life.

Kenner, Hugh, *The Pound Era;* Berkeley, University of California Press, 1971.
The modernist writers—Yeats, Joyce, Eliot, Pound, Wyndham Lewis—were all conservatives, a fact that has caused no little discomfiture to liberal critics; Kenner is one of their finest interpreters.

——*Wyndham Lewis: A Critical Guidebook;* New York, New Directions, 1954.

Wyndham Lewis was the scourge of Bloomsbury and the self-serving artistic establishment in England throughout his life, and he was a painter, critic, and novelist of the first rank; Kenner has done much to arouse interest in this fascinating, volcanic figure.

Kirk, Russell, *Eliot and His Age;* La Salle, IL, Sherwood Sugden, 1984.

Placing Eliot in philosophical and historical context, Kirk's book is not a work of literary criticism, but an elucidation of Eliot's writings in the light of moral and political wisdom.

——*Watchers at the Strait Gate;* Sauk City, WI, Arkham House, 1984.

An accomplished teller of ghostly tales, Kirk truly incorporates the "moral imagination" into his stories of purgatorial experience.

Koestler, Arthur, *Darkness at Noon;* New York, Bantam, 1970.

One of the most searing and penetrating political novels of this century; the protagonist is an old Bolshevik who relives his career under the brutal interrogation of his Stalinist captors.

Lewis, C.S., *An Experiment in Criticism;* Cambridge, Cambridge University Press, 1961.

In good reading, Lewis avers, we should be concerned less with altering our own opinions than in entering fully into the opinions of others.

——*The Discarded Image;* Cambridge, Cambridge University Press, 1964.

In this book Lewis recovers the medieval image of man and his world that gave to Western culture its imaginative order and splendor.

Lipman, Samuel, *The House of Music;* Boston, David R. Godine, 1984.
A "neoconservative" music critic's recent essays on the music scene in America and abroad.

Lytle, Andrew, *Stories: Alchemy and Others;* Sewanee, TN, University of the South Press, 1983.
One of the Southern Agrarians, Andrew Lytle's fiction has not received the critical attention it deserves; his vision is that of a Christian and a Southerner.

McInerny, Ralph, *The Noonday Devil;* New York, Atheneum, 1985.
A talented writer of mystery tales, McInerny has written several novels dealing with the state of the Catholic church in America; his orthodoxy provides him with critical insights, but his stories are tempered by a gentle irony.

Mencken, H.L., *Notes on Democracy;* reprinted, New York, Octagon Books, 1976.
Open up to almost any page Mencken ever wrote and you are more than likely to come across his particular blend of invective, satire, and buffoonery; here the complacent American pieties about democracy are chewed up and returned by Mencken to his readers.

Montgomery, Marion, *The Prophetic Poet and the Spirit of the Age,* 3 Vols; *Why Flannery O'Connor Stayed Home; Why Poe Drank Liquor; Why Hawthorne Was Melancholy;* La Salle, IL, Sherwood Sugden, 1981, 1983, 1984.
This is philosophical criticism and it isn't easy, but Montgomery's insights into the nature of modernity and the way the great American writers responded to it is a masterful

synthesis and an indispensable work of intellectual history.

O'Connor, Flannery, *The Complete Stories of Flannery O'Connor;* New York, Farrar, Straus and Giroux, 1971.
Many readers find the grotesque aspect of O'Connor's stories hard to swallow; yet it is essential to her vision, at once Catholic and Southern, which found the liberal belief in human perfectability to be disastrously naive.

Panichas, George, *The Reverent Discipline: Essays in Literary Criticism & Culture;* Knoxville, TN, University of Tennessee Press, 1974.
Literary critic and editor of *Modern Age,* Panichas insists that criticism has a moral imperative; these essays cover a range of literary topics, from Dostoevsky and Eliot to D.H. Lawrence and E.M. Forster.

——*The Courage of Judgment: Essays in Criticism, Culture & Society;* Knoxville, TN, University of Tennessee Press, 1982.
More essays, including some on the relation of religion and politics to literature.

Pei, Mario, *Double Speak in America;* New York, Hawthorn Books, 1975.
A leading author on the subject of language treats political jargon, especially liberal euphemism and gobbledygook, to a thorough examination.

Percy, Walker, *Lost in the Cosmos: The Last Self-Help Book;* New York, Farrar, Straus, Giroux, 1983.
Percy's novels embody his Catholic existentialist vision and are among the best by any living author; his two non-fiction books, including this latest, question the secular liberal ethos which he believes has resulted in sexual abuse,

growing violence, the worship of science and technology, and cultural triviality.

Podhoretz, Norman, *The Bloody Crossroads: Where Literature and Politics Meet;* New York, Simon and Schuster, 1986.
Though he has long been involved in debates over public policy, Podhoretz studied literature under Lionel Trilling; this collection of essays contains penetrating evaluations of such literary authors as Solzhenitsyn, Orwell, Camus, and others.

Simon, John, *Paradigms Lost: Literacy and Its Decline;* New York, Penguin, 1981.
In the tradition of Orwell, Simon laments the degeneration of language, seeing it as a breakdown in civility; this volume is mordant in tone and chock-full of examples.

——*Reverse Angle: American Film, 1970-1980;* New York, Crown, 1981.
Not much pleases the discriminating eye of John Simon, but given the quality of most films it is undoubtedly best to have a bouncer at the door of public taste.

——*Singularities: Essays on the Theater, 1964-1974;* New York, Random House, 1976.
More of the same, this time on the hapless Broadway stages.

Tate, Allen, *Essays of Four Decades;* Chicago, Swallow, 1969.
Poet, critic, novelist, man of letters, Tate was a modernist in literary style and a traditionalist in his political and religious sensibility.

Trilling, Lionel, *The Middle of the Journey;* New York, Harcourt, Brace, Jovanovich, 1980.
Along with Koestler's *Darkness At Noon,* this ranks as one of

the best political novels; intended to "draw out some of the moral and intellectual implications of the powerful attraction to Communism felt by . . . the American intellectual class during the Thirties and Forties." One of the characters is based on Whittaker Chambers.

Warren, Austin, *Rage for Order;* Ann Arbor, MI, University of Michigan Press, 1948.
Literary critic and Christian humanist, Warren here discusses such writers as George Herbert, Gerard Manley Hopkins, Yeats, Hawthorne, Kafka, Forster, and Henry James.

Wilder, Thornton, *The Eighth Day;* New York, Avon, 1976.
Though he is almost wholly known by his popular play, *Our Town,* Wilder wrote several novels of considerable power; they contain a vivid appreciation of traditional institutions and a profound moral sensitivity.

Wolfe, Tom, *Radical Chic and Mau-Mauing the Flak Catchers*; New York, Farrar, Straus and Giroux, 1970.
The leading practitioner of the New Journalism, Wolfe is perhaps the most scintillating cultural critic in America, especially when it comes to the pretensions of the liberal cultural elite; in "Radical Chic" he reveals the insanity of liberal guilt in the famous party held by Leonard Bernstein in honor of the Black Panthers.

——*The Purple Decades;* New York, Farrar, Straus, Giroux, 1984.
A collection of Wolfe's journalism which sparkles with his inimitable style.

Part II — Brief Lives of American Conservative Minds

The Founding and the Early Republic, 1763-1865

John Adams (1735-1826)

If John Adams's political fortunes were erratic and uncertain, his ideas and principles were strikingly consistent and powerfully expressed; with the possible exception of John C. Calhoun, they remain unequalled in American history. Trained as a lawyer, Adams was gifted with a legal and historical cast of mind: he understood that freedom consisted not in abstract, "natural" rights, but in the concrete institutions of a self-governing people. Though his Calvinism was diluted, his conviction that men were fallen and not amenable to infinite perfectability motivated his many attacks on the French *philosophes* and their American admirers, Jefferson included. Adams was a more moderate Federalist than Hamilton, insisting that a division and balancing of powers was necessary to restrain the passions both of potential tyrants and tyrannical mobs. With Burke, he was among the first political observers to thoroughly comprehend the threat of totalitarian ideologies; as a writer and as President, he helped to keep America free from those who wanted to import the French Revolution. However feisty he was in calling for American independence, Adams believed that an aristocracy of talent was natural to society and should be encouraged to offset the excesses of democracy. Only a virtuous people, Adams concluded, could govern themselves. And while he always retained a fierce pride in America, he never let it obscure the dangers that constantly assail a free people. See Peter Shaw, *The Character of John Ad-*

ams; New York, W.W. Norton, 1977; and Zoltan Haraszti, *John Adams and the Prophets of Progress;* New York, Grosset & Dunlap, 1952.

Defense of the Constitutions of Government of the United States of America; 3 vols.; reprinted, Adler, n.d.; *Discourses on Davila;* New York, Da Capo, 1973; *Political Writings of John Adams;* Indianapolis, IN, Bobbs-Merrill, 1954.

Fisher Ames (1758-1808)

The greatness of Fisher Ames lies not in his intellectual originality, but in his mastery of the word, both written and spoken, and in his statesmanship in the crucial years of George Washington's presidency. The leader of the Federalists in the first four sessions of Congress, Ames was instrumental in shaping the language of the First Amendment, and in marshalling support for the Federalist program. Yet he was not so much a politician, dealing in alliances and compromise, as an orator. From his youth, when he opposed an attempt in his home state of Massachusetts to impose a form of wage and price controls, to his final years of ill-health and withdrawal, Ames upheld a Burkean conservatism that saw the "democracy" of the French Revolution as an ideological threat to ordered liberty. Long before anyone coined the term "media" Ames was deriding the notion that "public opinion" would guarantee the triumph of reason. Only a virtuous people, led by an aristocracy of talent, could live up to the ideals set forth in the Constitution. Though now an obscure figure, Ames's writings read with a vitality and "relevance" almost unequalled among his contemporaries. See William B. Allen's introduction to the Liberty Classics edition of Ames's *Works* and also Winfred E.A. Bernhard's *Fisher Ames: Federalist and Statesman;* Chapel Hill, NC, University of North Carolina Press, 1965.

Works of Fisher Ames; 2 vols.; Indianapolis, IN, Liberty Press, 1983.

Orestes Brownson (1803-1876)

Orestes Brownson's contemporaries called him a "weather-vane" because he seemed to change his religious and political alliances every two years. He had embraced Congregational-ism, Presbyterianism, Universalism, socialism, atheism, and Unitarianism, each time expounding his position with a reck-less enthusiasm that generated not only irritation but respect and attention. But a definite logic ran through Brownson's search: he sought a religious authority that proclaimed moral absolutes and commanded obedience, thus providing the moral foundation for a free society. This he found in the Ro-man Catholic Church, whose leading cultural defender he be-came in the middle decades of the nineteenth century. Foreshadowing the major role Catholicism would have in twentieth century conservatism, Brownson held that the American Republic could cohere only when the people were not indulging in the willfulness and caprice of private judg-ment. The political analogy of private judgment was mob de-mocracy, where the people manipulated the government to cater to their wishes. Brownson's solution to the problem of authority was certainly unique: he believed that a nation which obeyed the moral authority of the Catholic Church would be freed to pursue the common good. Contrary to the allegations against him, Brownson did not want to alter the Constitution, which he thought best suited America's histori-cal situation. His classic work is *The American Republic*. See Thomas R. Ryan, *Orestes A. Brownson;* Huntington, IN, Our Sunday Visitor, 1976.

The American Republic; New Haven, CT, College and Univer-sity Press, 1972; *Works;* 20 vols.; reprinted, New York, AMS Press, n.d.

John C. Calhoun (1782-1851)

It is now standard practice in the textbooks to picture John C.

Calhoun as the evil Southerner who caused the Civil War. Putting aside the debates about that conflict, it is nevertheless ironic that the profoundest political thinker on the subject of the rights of minorities should be caricatured by liberal ideologues. For Calhoun's ideas transcend their time and speak to our own situation with a startling relevance. Thanks to the instrument of the welfare state and the language of "rights," America has become dominated by the incessant demands of "minorities" and "special interest groups." This divisiveness, in which the most powerful lobbies can guarantee their demands, causes the breakup of a national consensus, where the needs of a group are to be seen in the light of the common good. His central idea of the "concurrent majority" recognized the diversity of "interests," and held that they should be taken into account in order that a compromise, or consensus, could be reached. In this way no minority would be trampled under foot; diversity would be preserved from a tyrannical uniformity. As the great Southerners, and Calhoun among them, have reminded us, true nationalism springs from a love of one's own region. Calhoun's political thought is rich and compelling; perhaps Americans will return to it when they sense the danger posed by a nation of warring factions. See August O. Spain, *The Political Theory of John C. Calhoun;* New York, Octagon Books, 1951.

Calhoun: Basic Documents; State College, PA, Pennsylvania State University Press, 1952; *A Disquisition on Government;* Gloucester, MA, Peter Smith, 1958; *The Papers of John C. Calhoun;* Columbia, SC, University of South Carolina Press.

James Fenimore Cooper (1789-1851)

James Fenimore Cooper always defended America while in Europe, but he was its toughest critic while at home. Known primarily for his Leatherstocking novels, Cooper actually wrote widely on political and historical subjects, partly as an outgrowth of his European travels. He attempted a few political novels, but these were neither good fiction nor social criticism: *The American Democrat* remains the best distillation of his political ideas. Here he champions the freedom and dignity which democracy allows while warning that abstract equality and liberty are not attainable. A democracy can flourish only when its leaders are gentlemen. The gentleman is not defined by wealth primarily (though Cooper vigorously defended property rights), but by his culture, public spiritedness, and prudence. To rely on public opinion, as moulded by the popular press, instead of the hard truth self-government requires, is fatuous, since that press thrives on resentment and emotionalism. If Cooper's specifically political novels are justly neglected, his Leatherstocking tales are shot through with the essential themes confronting the young American republic: the individual vs. the community, law vs. will, exclusivism vs. diversity. In these novels Cooper achieves a fully dramatic enactment of the ideas which preoccupied him. See the introduction to the Liberty Classics edition of *The American Democrat*.

The American Democrat; Indianapolis, IN, Liberty Classics, 1981.

John Dickinson (1732-1808)

Nowhere is the conservative assertion that the American Revolution was a preservation of a traditional order rather than a radical restructuring of political society more evident than in the life and writings of John Dickinson. A Philadelphia lawyer educated at the Middle Temple in London, Dickinson participated in most of the crucial events of the Founding era from the Stamp Act Congress to the Constitutional Convention. His *Letters from a Farmer in Pennsylvania* placed the dispute with England in historical and constitutional context for most Americans. Unlike the abstract doctrines of "rights" formulated by Thomas Paine, Dickinson's political sensibility was based on history and precedent. "Experience must be our only guide," Dickinson stated. "Reason may mislead us." Dickinson believed in a government of laws, the rules which enable men to pursue virtue. Central to his understanding of politics was the distinction between government and society; government does not exist to achieve ends but to free men to choose their own ends. See the chapter on Dickinson in M.E. Bradford's *A Better Guide Than Reason: Studies in the American Revolution;* La Salle, IL, Sherwood Sugden, 1979.

The Political Writings of John Dickinson, 1764-1774; New York, Da Capo, 1970.

Alexander Hamilton (1757-1804)

Conservatives have always been divided over whether to see Alexander Hamilton as a legitimate progenitor. That he was a man out of his time and place few would dispute: born outside the Colonies, he never had an adequate understanding of American localism and the prerogatives of the states; enamored of England's unified political and banking systems, he hoped to create a mercantilist commercial republic. It was Adam Smith, not Hamilton, who would undergird conservative economics. Yet it must be said that Hamilton played a central role, as the most prolific author of *The Federalist,* and as a persuasive voice at the New York ratifying convention, in the adoption of the Constitution. Though a proponent of the centralized state, he sought a power strong enough to avoid the peril of mob democracy. His strictures against the French Revolution were sincere and effective. And his vision of America as a prosperous, independent commercial power has been fulfilled, albeit in ways he might not have expected. See Forrest McDonald's *Alexander Hamilton: A Biography;* New York, W.W. Norton, 1979.

Selected Writings and Speeches of Alexander Hamilton; American Enterprise Institute, Washington, DC, 1985; *The Federalist;* New York, Bantam, 1982; *The Papers of Alexander Hamilton;* 26 vols.; New York, Columbia University Press, 1961-1978.

Nathaniel Hawthorne (1804-1864)

At a time when the New England mind was dominated by the Transcendentalists, with their religion of humanity, their utopian communities and schemes of social improvement, Hawthorne stood apart as the dark romancer of sin and hypocrisy. Hawthorne's imagination was preoccupied with the past, which he saw as a living thing that continues to shape us, whether we remember it or not. His political interests were marked by prudence and common sense, but his lasting conservative influence stems from his fiction. *The Blithedale Romance* is a complex and ultimately damning story based on the utopian community of Brook Farm. And in such tales as "Earth's Holocaust," "The Celestial Railroad," and "The Hall of Fantasy," Hawthorne satirizes the belief that we can throw off the past, and even our human nature, in pursuit of social experiments. Of course, Hawthorne's friend, Herman Melville, also possessed an essentially conservative imagination, and though his art is full of ambiguity, it contains a profound commentary on his times. A difficult but rewarding study of Hawthorne is Marion Montgomery's *Why Hawthorne Was Melancholy;* La Salle, IL, Sherwood Sugden, 1984.

The Blithedale Romance; New York, Penguin, 1985; *The Scarlet Letter and Selected Tales;* New York, Penguin.

James Kent (1763-1847)

Along with Joseph Story (see below), Chancellor Kent became

one of the most influential jurists and commentators on constitutional law, largely through his formative impact on generations of American lawyers. A staunch defender of the common law, and its roots in the natural law, Kent once wrote: "The law, as a science, is only a collection of general principles, founded on the moral law, and in the common sense of mankind, and applied to particular cases as they arise, by the diligence of the bar and the erudition of the courts."

Commentaries on American Law; 4 vols., 1826; reprinted, New York, Da Capo, 1971.

James Madison (1750/51-1836)

"In framing a government which is to be administered by men over men, the great difficulty lies in this: you must first enable the government to control the governed; and in the next place oblige it to control itself." These famous conservative words belong to James Madison, contributor to *The Federalist,* leader at the Constitutional Convention, and fourth President of the United States. Madison's political ideas and opinions underwent many shifts, but his essential conservatism has been ignored by left-leaning academics. By taking his ideas out of context and substituting a modern meaning for words meant very differently, liberals have made James Madison out to be a champion of "natural rights" and the exclusion of religion from public life. Madison's attitude toward the Bill of Rights was restrained: he saw it as a compromise with the Anti-Federalists, and certainly not a blueprint for the reordering of American society. The central thrust of his politics was on the separation and balancing of governmental powers. Despite the assertions that Madison was a mild Hobbesian who only believed that men's passions would offset each other in an ingeniously contrived system, this statesman put his hope in the "third force" of virtuous representatives who would arrive at the "deliberate sense of the community." What he feared above all was the "majority faction" that would sweep through the states and place an ideological group in power. Thanks to his efforts, this has never taken place. See M.E. Bradford's chapter on Madison in *A Worthy Company;* Marlborough, NH, 1982, and also the chapter on "The Two Majorities in American Politics" in Willmoore Kendall's *The Conservative Affirmation;* Chicago, Regnery Gateway, 1985.

The Forging of American Federalism: Selected Writings of James Madison; New York, Harper Torchbooks, 1965; *The Federalist Papers;* New York, Bantam, 1982.

John Randolph of Roanoke (1773-1833)

Fiery, eccentric, proud, and eloquent, John Randolph of Roanoke never hesitated to sacrifice popularity or power to the claims of truth as he saw them. At a time when the centralized edifice created by the Federalists threatened to become an activist state, with "internal improvements," discriminatory tariffs, and standing armies, Randolph railed against the modern temptation to meddle with the social fabric. Deeply attached to the local communities of his state of Virginia, Randolph feared the collapsing of the states into an amorphous national democracy ruled by "King Numbers." But if Randolph abhorred the Federalists with their national and commercial vision, he also rejected the Rousseauistic talk of the "rights of man" in which Jefferson had indulged. Society cannot be created out of nothing; it is an organic development; to pull up its roots is to invite anarchy. Envy and a lust for power drive men to reject the natural hierarchies and call for a democracy based on notions of absolute "equality." Far from freeing men, egalitarianism sets them at each other's throats. Randolph's voice soon was drowned out by men like Andrew Jackson (whose slogan was "the supremacy of the people's will"), but his principles would inform men like Calhoun and conservatives beyond the South. See Russell Kirk, *John Randolph of Roanoke;* Indianapolis, IN, Liberty Press, 1978.

Most of Randolph's speeches and letters remain uncollected, but several major speeches are gathered at the end of Kirk's book, cited above.

Joseph Story (1779-1845)

Overshadowed by the almost larger-than-life figure of Chief Justice John Marshall, Joseph Story, Associate Justice of the Supreme Court from 1811 to 1845, has an equal claim to having influenced the American study and understanding of constitutional law. Recent research has suggested that Story was a major influence on both Marshall and Daniel Webster. His monumental work, *Commentaries on the Constitution,* became a universal textbook for young American lawyers. Story's achievement lay in his thorough knowledge of the common law, especially as it developed in England. Steeped in Burke and Paley, Story rejected the Lockean theory of natural "rights." The common law, as it embodies the natural law, "is that system of principles, which human reason has discovered to regulate the conduct of man. . . . In its largest sense, it comprehends natural theology, moral philosophy, and political philosophy . . . it comprehends man's duties to God, to himself, to other men, and as a member of political society." A stern opponent of mob democracy, Story's strong nationalism is said to have partly polarized the debate leading up to the Civil War. For a thorough evaluation of Story, see James McClellan's *Joseph Story and the American Constitution;* Norman, OK, University of Oklahoma Press, 1971.

Commentaries on the Constitution of the United States; Boston, Little, Brown, 1873; *Commentaries on Equity Jurisprudence;* 2 vols., 1836; New York, Arno, 1972; *The Miscellaneous Writings of Joseph Story;* New York, Da Capo, 1972.

John Taylor of Caroline (1753-1824)

With John Randolph of Roanoke, the Virginia planter-aristocrat, John Taylor of Caroline, became a leader of the Anti-Federalists. Though he carried on a debate with John Adams (a statesman and political thinker he admired) he opposed not the higher aspirations of men like Adams, but the commercial and sectional motives of less honorable Federalists. Taylor believed that the Constitution existed to protect the powers of the states; he saw it as an attempt to forestall any domination of the British kind, where an external government would impose its self-interested dictates. A prototype of the Southern conservative, Taylor cherished the hierarchical, agrarian community, bound by custom, religion, and manners. Above all, he feared a society which sought to fulfill abstract notions of "rights" or economic gain. Like future Southerners, Taylor, who participated in politics only in brief intervals, insisted on the distinctness of the public and private realms. The role of government is to administer laws, not to achieve some vision of "social justice." See M.E. Bradford's introduction to the Liberty Press edition of *Arator* and also Eugene T. Mudge, *The Social Philosophy of John Taylor of Caroline;* New York, AMS Press, 1968.

Arator: Being a Series of Agricultural Essays; Indianapolis, IN, Liberty Classics, 1977; *Construction Construed, and Constitutions Vindicated;* New York, Da Capo, 1970; *New Views of the Constitution of the United States;* New York, Da Capo, 1971.

Between the Wars, 1865-1945

Brooks Adams (1848-1927)

Brooks Adams cannot be classified as a conservative, strictly speaking. His ideas were often paradoxical, perhaps more often confused. Like his brother Henry, he saw decay, chaos, and unrestricted passion in the social scene: the capitalist class, far from establishing a law-abiding and orderly system, pursues ruthless competition, using its immense power to trample over the laws. The centrifugal force of capitalism threatens a complete breakdown of society into a new barbarism; Brooks Adams believed that only centralized administration could hold America together. He admitted that the only vestige of his Calvinist heritage lay in his determinism: with Marx, he foresaw the triumph of brute social and historical forces. Yet he was an astute and occasionally prophetic critic of urban political corruption, overweening businessmen, and the Machiavellianism which masqueraded as "democracy." See the section on Brooks Adams in Russell Kirk's *The Conservative Mind.*

The Law of Civilization and Decay; New York, Arno, 1955; *The New Empire;* New Brunswick, NJ, Transaction Books, 1983; *America's Economic Supremacy;* Freeport, Books for Libraries Press, 1971.

Henry Adams (1838-1918)

Like his brother Brooks, Henry Adams was convinced that the scientific laws of history were leading mankind inevitably to decay, and yet he gave eloquent testimony to the institutions and beliefs that gave Western civilization an unparalleled level of order and beauty. Adams studied Mill, Comte, and Darwin, but only took scattered insights from them; his political understanding was nourished by a deep reading of Tocqueville and an intimate knowledge of his grandfather's and great-grandfather's statecraft. Adams went back to the medieval age to find an era that had combined power with grace; he found that combination in the Virgin. But modern times, he thought, were dominated by brute force, symbolized by the Dynamo; men were increasingly the victims of their own growing mastery of nature. In politics, the rule of demagogues and self-interested capitalists mirrored the new order of raw power. Looking back to the early American republic, Adams saw no evolutionary progression to the present, but a sad decline from his ancestor John Adams to the tawdry politics of General Grant. Henry Adams could not find faith in the Virgin and her Son; he remained a detached, mordant observer, equally scornful of arrogant businessmen and socialist bureaucracy. His prophecy of a major cataclysm came true in World War I, and twentieth century politics were indeed to be overshadowed by a totalitarian use of power. See W.H. Jordy, *Henry Adams: Scientific Historian;* New Haven, Shoe String Press, 1970.

History of the United States of America During the Administrations of Jefferson and Madison; Chicago, University of Chicago Press, 1979; *The Education of Henry Adams;* Boston, Houghton Mifflin, 1973; *Democracy: A Novel;* New York, Crown, 1982; *The Degradation of the Democratic Dogma;* Gloucester, MA, Peter Smith, n.d.; *Mont Saint-Michel and Chartres;* Princeton, Princeton University Press, 1981.

Irving Babbitt (1865-1933)

"As against expansionists of every kind, I do not hesitate to affirm that what is specifically human in man and ultimately divine is a certain quality of will, a will that is felt in its relation to his ordinary self as a will to refrain." Irving Babbitt lived during a time of expansionism: not only economic and geographical expansionism, but the kind of progressivism which posited man's perfectability through technology and social planning. As the leader of the New Humanism, Babbitt upheld not a secular mentality (as the word "humanism" has come to mean), but a moral discipline. He was convinced that Bacon and Rousseau were the great anti-humanists: the scientism of Bacon led inevitably to the sentimental dreams of Rousseau. In society and in art, Babbitt demonstrated, self-indulgence leads to anarchy and meaninglessness. The Western cultural heritage, resting on the wisdom of philosophers like Plato and St. Augustine, has insisted that man's reason must control his appetites. Knowing man's limitations is the best antidote to utopian schemes. Babbitt, an erudite scholar, also found in the East a religious tradition to support his contentions. Babbitt was a Harvard professor, but he scorned the "ivory tower" and was one of the first conservatives to condemn the "treason" of the intellectuals who had abandoned reality and immersed themselves in ideology. See George A. Panichas and Claes G. Ryn, eds., *Irving Babbitt in Our Time;* Washington, DC: Catholic University Press, 1986, and J. David Hoeveler, *The New Humanism: A Critique of Modern America, 1900-1940;* Charlottesville, VA, University of Virginia Press, 1977.

Democracy and Leadership; Indianapolis, IN, Liberty Classics, 1979; *Literature and the American College;* Clifton, NJ, Kelley, 1972; *Rousseau and Romanticism;* Austin, TX, University of Texas Press, 1977; *Irving Babbitt: Representative Writings;* Lincoln, NE, University of Nebraska Press, 1981.

E.L. Godkin (1831-1902)

It may be hard to believe, but there was a time when the *Nation* was not the voice of self-righteous socialism. When English-born E.L. Godkin edited the *Nation* in the latter part of the nineteenth century, it was an exponent of classical liberalism, attacking the vulgarity of the Gilded Age while upholding the free market, and calling for democratic reforms while pillorying the mediocrity and corruption of democratic institutions. Godkin's main contributions were his critique of the "yellow journalism" which went hand-in-hand with the degradation of the democratic dogma, and his defense of property and economic initiative against the lures of state intervention. See the section on Godkin in Russell Kirk's *The Conservative Mind.*

Unforeseen Tendencies of Democracy; New York, Arno, n.d.

H.L. Mencken (1880-1956)

H.L. Mencken's wit was so acidic that it not only cut through whatever he applied it to, it tended to leave nothing behind. The leading journalist in the first half of this century, Mencken worked at the *Baltimore Sun* when that city was at its height. If he had any philosophical base, it would be more "libertarian" than conservative. In *Notes on Democracy,* Mencken punctured many of America's preciously held illusions about the will of the people. He was the founder of *The American Mercury,* a sophisticated journal where much of the best conservative writing appeared in the 1920s and 1930s.

The American Language; New York, Knopf, 1977; *Notes on Democracy;* New York, Octagon, 1976; *Prejudices;* 6 vols.; New York, Octagon, 1976; *The American Scene: A Reader;* New York, Knopf, 1965; *Treatise on Right and Wrong;* New York, Octagon, 1976.

Paul Elmer More (1867-1937)

"The greatest of our intellectual conservatives"; "the greatest of American critics": so Francis G. Wilson and Russell Kirk have characterized Paul Elmer More. With Irving Babbitt, More was responsible for establishing the vigorous conservative movement known as the "New Humanism." More was a man of letters in the true sense: he was an editor of *The Nation,* a literary critic, historian of Greek culture, and an Anglican apologist for orthodox Christianity. Originally a skeptic, More's study of Plato's dualistic concepts of spirit and matter, good and evil, led him to Christianity and the conviction that moral and political order cannot last without religious foundations. Relentlessly he stripped away the sentimental and unrealistic elements of liberal humanitarianism to reveal the ideological will to restructure society and even human nature itself. More unabashedly claimed that democracy needed to be leavened by an aristocracy of just men, and he asserted that private property was the single most civilizing force in the life of a nation. Going beyond the more generalized religious ideas of Babbitt, More stressed the centrality of the Incarnation to our understanding of man and God, and he eloquently rebutted the modernists of his day who were busy reducing revelation to myth and psychology. As a literary critic of the first rank, More upheld the moral imagination; many of his interpretations anticipated more recent judgments. As a Christian scholar of wide reading and historical sensitivity, More became a model of the conservative intellectual. See J. David Hoeveler, *The New Humanism: A Critique of Modern America, 1900-1940;* Charlottesville, VA, University of Virginia Press, 1977.

Shelburne Essays; 11 vols.; reprinted, Phaeton, 1967; *The Religion of Plato;* Millwood, NY, Kraus, n.d.; *Shelburne Essays: Second Series;* Millwood, NY, Kraus, n.d.; *Platonism;* New York, Greenwood Press, 1969; *The Catholic Faith;* Port Washington, NY, Kennikat, 1971; *Hellenistic Philosophies;* New York, Greenwood Press, n.d.

Albert Jay Nock (1870-1945)

"If we look beneath the surface of our public affairs, we can discern one fundamental fact, namely: a great redistribution of power between society and the State." So opens *Our Enemy, The State* by Albert Jay Nock, an enigmatic but compelling writer of biography, political analysis, and literary criticism whose works influenced many of the leading figures of the post-World War II conservative intellectual movement. Nock was not a systematic thinker: he was influenced by such diverse writers as Rabelais, Artemus Ward, Jefferson, and Henry George. From George he took the important distinction between society and the State. According to Nock, the State is a perversion of government: it goes beyond the functions of benevolent policeman, and arrogates to itself the right to direct human affairs. Nock was an individualist to the core and believed that men should take responsibility for themselves rather than for others. Taking the idea from Isaiah, Nock held that a "remnant" of conservative individualists would be the hope of a free society. For all his fierce dislike of government, Nock was not a partisan of what he called "economism"; he espoused a more classical definition of culture and art. See Robert M. Crunden, *The Mind and Art of Albert Jay Nock;* Chicago, Henry Regnery, 1964.

Our Enemy, The State; New York, Arno, 1972; *Memoirs of a Superfluous Man;* Chicago, Regnery Gateway, 1978.

Agnes Repplier (1855-1950)

That women may seem woefully underrepresented in this sourcebook is partly due to its restricted scope, for outstanding conservative women have not been lacking in America. These women, however, have largely been oriented to literature rather than to politics. Acute observers of social change and of the strain on traditional institutions and mores, these writers have included Ellen Glasgow, Edith Wharton, Willa Cather, and Phyllis McGinley. Each of them deserves, and repays, careful reading. Agnes Repplier has been chosen because as the "dean of American essayists" for nearly half a century, she injected her witty, ironic, conservatism into the discussion of literature and manners. Equally scornful of American imperialism and of collectivist fantasies, she combined a brisk, almost modern, temperament with a profound attachment to the enduring legacy of Western civilization. "It is well that the past yields some solace to the temperamental conservative, for the present is his only on terms he cannot easily fulfill. . . . He is powerless to deny the existence of facts he does not like. He is powerless to credit new systems with finality. The sanguine assurance that men and nations can be legislated into goodness, that pressure from without is equivalent to moral change from within, needs a strong backing of inexperience." See the splendid chapter—part biography, part panegyric, part chrestomathy—on Repplier in John Lukacs's *Philadelphia, 1900-1950: Patricians and Philistines;* New York, Farrar, Straus & Giroux, 1981.

Eight Decades (essays); Port Washington, NY, Kennikat, 1970.

George Santayana (1863-1952)

Like so many conservatives, George Santayana cannot easily be fitted into a mould. Proud of his Spanish origins, he combined an aesthetic traditionalism with the tough philosophical materialism and skepticism of New England, where he spent forty years of his life. A professor of philosophy at Harvard for a time, Santayana eventually withdrew to Europe to cultivate his critique of modern society. At a time when industrialism and pragmatism were in the ascendency, he held that the common good lay not in the gross national product but in the life of art and culture. True individualism, he declared, stemmed from a knowledge of the past, the beautiful, and human limitations. Santayana saw through the cult of "democracy," which he believed to be the result of false individualism, producing a mass of isolated atoms, held together only by economic motives.

141

Perhaps his profoundest contribution to conservative thought was his analysis of the legacy of classical liberalism. What began with an "enlightened" desire to allow a maximum of liberty in which old mores and institutions were relaxed (the first attempt at "pluralism"), ended in a tyrannical regime. The liberal inevitably becomes the reformer, embodying a "Will" which cannot allow any other source of authority. Santayana prophetically foresaw the paradox of liberalism which is now being acted out in America: a self-proclaimed belief in pluralism that coexists with an intolerance of traditional institutions and beliefs. For an excellent overview of Santayana's thought, see Russell Kirk's *The Conservative Mind.*

Character and Opinion in the United States; New York, W.W. Norton, 1967; *Dominations & Powers: Reflections on Liberty, Society and Government;* New York, Scribner's, 1951; *The Last Puritan;* New York, Scribner's, 1935; *Winds of Doctrine & Platonism & the Spiritual Life;* Gloucester, MA, Peter Smith, 1958; *Persons and Places;* 3 vols.; New York, 1944, 1953; *Selected Critical Writings;* Cambridge, Cambridge University Press, 1968.

William Graham Sumner (1840-1910)

Sumner is routinely characterized by intellectual historians as a late nineteenth century apologist for Robber Barons, Big Business, and Social Darwinism. But this is a false picture of a complex and independent thinker. It is true that Sumner was an iconoclastic disciple of Darwin and the English sociologist Herbert Spencer (the founder of "Social Darwinism"), and that he espoused the "scientific" view of man. Yet his defense of the free market unencumbered by government intervention was based on a belief that American liberty was derived from the hard work of self-sufficient individuals. Sumner was a pugnacious opponent not only of the state, but of the protective measures sought by big business, including the tariff and government-sponsored monopolies. His attack on the popular American imperialism of the Spanish-American war was unflinching. He was keenly aware of the tendency towards politicization, whether it was the incipient glorification of "democracy" (which he saw as a euphemism for crass electioneering), the pressure for a welfare state, or the self-interestedness of large corporations. Toward the end of his life he became bitter, predicting a future of "war, debt, taxation, diplomacy, a grand governmental system, pomp, glory, a big army and navy, lavish expenditures, political jobbery." Whatever his failings, Sumner was a unique conservative voice. See the introduction to the Gateway edition of his *The Conquest of the United States by Spain and Other Essays.*

The Conquest of the United States by Spain and Other Essays; Chicago, Henry Regnery; *Essays of William Graham Sumner;* 1934; reprinted, Hamden, CT, Shoe String Press, 1969; *What Social Classes Owe to Each Other;* Caldwell, ID, Caxton, 1947.

Conservatism Redivivus, 1945-1985

Walter Berns (1919-)

A student of political philosopher Leo Strauss, Walter Berns is a conservative constitutional scholar who received public attention in the late 1960s for resigning from the Cornell University faculty in protest at the university's craven capitulation to student violence and radical activism. Berns has been a persistent critic of the liberal interpretations of the Constitution as a document without specific "meaning" intended by the Founders—in short, as a palimpsest upon which each generation can superimpose its own particular desires. Rejecting the liberal belief, inherited from J.S. Mill, that "truth" will inevitably win out in a "pluralistic" society, Berns holds that the end of law is to inculcate virtue in the citizenry. Some of the issues Berns has written extensively about are the scope of the First Amendment, the need for censorship of pornography, and the legitimacy of capital punishment.

Freedom, Virtue, and the First Amendment; 1957; reprinted, New York, Greenwood Press, 1969; *The First Amendment and the Future of American Democracy;* New York, Basic Books, 1975; *Capital Punishment: Crime and the Morality of the Death Penalty;* New York, Basic Books, 1979; *In Defense of Liberal Democracy;* Chicago, Regnery/Gateway, 1985.

L. Brent Bozell (1925-)

Mercurial but thoughtful, uncompromising in debates touching upon first principles, L. Brent Bozell has left an indelible impression on the conservative movement. With his brother-in-law, William F. Buckley, Jr., Bozell authored *McCarthy and His Enemies,* which asserted the reality of Communist subversion and the right of Congress to investigate such treasonous activities. As an able polemicist and activist, Bozell helped to pull the Republican Party to the Right—a direction which, with occasionally faltering steps, it has continued to travel. Bozell's *The Warren Revolution* was a major conservative response to the judicial activism of the New Deal era, and an immediate reaction to the controversial *Brown v. Board of Education* decision. A convert to the Roman Catholic church, Bozell founded and edited a conservative, Catholic magazine called *Triumph* which developed an extreme traditionalist position. Disturbed by abortion, permissiveness, and liberal legislation, Bozell diverged from the arguments of Willmoore Kendall and John Courtney Murray, which asserted the harmony of America's natural law tradition with Catholicism, and upheld a Continental, and particularly Spanish, model of a Christian commonwealth. Bozell's extremism separated him from most conservatives, but like many extremists, his criticisms of society have often been prescient.

With William F. Buckley, Jr., *McCarthy and His Enemies;* 1954; reprinted, New Rochelle, NY, Arlington House, 1980; *The Warren Revolution;* New Rochelle, NY, Arlington House, 1966.

William F. Buckley, Jr. (1925-)

From the *enfant terrible* of *God and Man at Yale* to the conservative pundit of *National Review* and *Firing Line* to a fixture on the American cultural landscape as the author of popular spy novels and friend and advisor to a sitting President of the United States, the career of William F. Buckley, Jr. has paralleled and reflected the maturing conservative intellectual movement in America. After blasting his alma mater for hypocritically endorsing God and free enterprise while hiring professors who taught atheism and socialism, Buckley turned to the mounting tensions surrounding Senator McCarthy. With his brother-in-law, L. Brent Bozell, he wrote *McCarthy and His Enemies,* which cut through the hysteria on both sides to focus on a single question: was there indeed extensive Communist infiltration of the U.S. Government? The authors concluded that there was, and that such a phenomenon had to be confronted. Drawing on a remarkable number of brilliant conservative minds, including William Schlamm, Frank Meyer, Willmoore Kendall, and James Burnham, Buckley gave conservatives a national voice when he founded *National Review* in 1955. In the internal debates of conservatism over the years, Buckley often embodied both sides in himself, such as the traditional vs. the libertarian, or the isolationist vs. the internationalist. Through the force of his personality and his ability to find a workable center, Buckley helped to hold the movement together and weld it into a formidable influence in the national debate. His urbanity, culture, and ability to provoke discussion have provided conservatism with a respectability (for lack of a better word) that it might not otherwise have had. More than one wag has said that if William F. Buckley, Jr. didn't exist, it would be necessary to invent him.

God and Man at Yale; 1951; reprinted, Chicago, Regnery/Gateway, 1977; with L. Brent Bozell, *McCarthy and His Enemies;* 1954; reprinted, New Rochelle, NY, Arlington House, 1980; *The Jeweler's Eye;* New York, G.P. Putnam, 1958; *Up From Liberalism;* 1959; reprinted, New York, Stein & Day, 1985; ed., *The Committee and Its Critics;* New York, G.P. Putnam, 1962; *The Governor Listeth;* New York, G.P. Putnam, 1963; *Rumbles Left and Right;* New York, G.P. Putnam, 1963; *The Unmaking of a Mayor;* 1966; reprinted, New Rochelle, NY, Arlington House, 1977; *Inveighing We Will Go;* New York, G.P. Putnam, 1969; ed., *Did You Ever See a Dream Walking?*

American Conservative Thought in the Twentieth Century; In-dianapolis, IN, Bobbs-Merrill, 1970; ed., *Odyssey of a Friend;* New York, G.P. Putnam, 1970; *Cruising Speed;* New York, G.P. Putnam, 1969; *Four Reforms;* New York, G.P. Putnam, 1973; *United Nations Journal: A Delegate's Odyssey;* New York, G.P. Putnam, 1974; *Execution Eve;* New York, G.P. Putnam, 1975; *A Hymnal: The Controversial Arts;* New York, G.P. Putnam, 1978; *Overdrive;* Garden City, NY, Doubleday, 1983; *Right Reason;* New York, Doubleday, 1985.

James Burnham (1905-)

For his dispassionate realism, his insight into the threat posed to the free world by the Soviet empire, and his commitment to doing what is necessary to preserve the West, James Burnham can justly be ranked as one of the towering intellects of this century. A Trotskyist in the 1930s, and active in Communist circles, Burnham underwent a steady disillusionment (he called it a "reeducation"), though he continued to associate with the Left, including the *Partisan Review* crowd. In 1941 he published *The Managerial Revolution,* which predicted the growth of government by non-ideological bureaucracies, and which influenced George Orwell profoundly. Burnham turned to the global challenge of Communism in the following years; with inexorable logic, he proved the inadequacy of the "containment" doctrine in the face of the Soviet objective of world domination. A thoroughgoing interventionist, Burnham advocated anti-Communist subversion and propaganda, call-ing for direct military involvement in the Hungarian uprising of 1956 and the training of exiles for wars of liberation. In two seminal works, Burnham displayed his intellectual versatility. In *Congress and the American Tradition* he warned of the de-velopment of the "imperial presidency," and the dangers of the liberal attempt to embody the "will of the people" through more "direct" channels than the deliberations of Congress. Burnham saw in liberalism a secular, progressivist faith in the malleability of man. With Whittaker Chambers he knew this faith to be ultimately the same as that of Communism—hence liberalism's inability to stand up to the Soviet threat. Willing to dispense with the restraints on the passions which traditional classical and Christian thought knew to be necessary safeguards to freedom, liberalism inevitably opened the door to tyranny. Burnham's analysis of liberalism was fully elaborated in *Suicide of the West,* a book which has lost none of its astringent power. The best study of Burnham is by Samuel T. Francis, *Power and History: The Political Thought of James Burnham;* Lanham, MD, University Press of America, 1984.

The Managerial Revolution; 1941; reprinted, New York, Greenwood Press, 1972; *The Machiavellians: Defenders of Freedom;* 1943; reprinted, Regnery/Gateway, 1962; *The Struggle for the World;* New York, John Day, 1954; *The Coming Defeat of Communism;* 1950; reprinted, New York, Greenwood Press, 1968; *Containment or Liberation?;* New York, John Day, 1953; *The Web of Subversion;* New York, John Day, 1954; *Congress and the American Tradition;* Chicago, Henry Regnery, 1959; *Suicide of the West: The Meaning and Destiny of Liberalism;* 1964; reprinted, Regnery/Gateway, 1985; *The War We Are In;* New Rochelle, NY, Arlington House, 1967.

John Chamberlain (1903-)

John Chamberlain's half century as a journalist has been marked by a consistently fair-minded, but thoroughly principled, approach to the issues of the day. Like so many of his generation, Chamberlain abandoned his youthful leftism and came to a renewed appreciation of America's tradition of individual liberty. Chamberlain's position can be described as "libertarian," but in perhaps a deeper sense he is an "individualist," one who deplores the tendency of collectivism to diminish human creativity and responsibility. After working for *Time* and *The New York Times,* Chamberlain became a co-editor of *The Freeman,* a journal to which he still contributes. The books he has written on the nature and history of capitalism are considered models of lucidity and balance. William F. Buckley, Jr. has characterized Chamberlain's gifts: "The voice of reason, from an affable man; unacquainted with affectation; deeply committed to the cause of his country . . . ."

Farewell to Reform: The Rise, Life & Decay of the Progressive Mind in America; 1932; reprinted, Gloucester, MA, Peter Smith, 1958; *John Dos Passos: A Biographical and Critical Essay;* New York, Harcourt, Brace and World, 1939; ed., *The National Review Reader;* New York, Bookmailer, 1957; *The Roots of Capitalism;* 1959; reprinted, Indianapolis, IN, Liberty Press, 1977; *The Enterprising Americans: A Business History of the United States;* 1963; rev. ed., New York, Harper & Row, 1974; *A Life With the Printed Word;* Chicago, Regnery/Gateway, 1982.

William Henry Chamberlin (1897-1969)

A journalist of uncommon integrity and insight, William Henry Chamberlin, in his evolving case for conservatism, embodied the inner conflicts and search for common principles that marked the conservative movement in the 1940s and 1950s. Having witnessed Soviet totalitarianism for himself while on assignment in the 1930s, Chamberlin became an articulate defender of America's tradition of democratic capitalism. He was one of the founders of *Human Events* and shaped its approach to foreign policy issues. Chamberlin was deeply disturbed by Franklin Roosevelt's handling of World War II, and by the facile adulation of the Soviet "ally." With *America's Second Crusade* he became one of the first "revisionist" historians of the war, and began to abandon his isolationist leanings for a more vigorous anti-Communist position. He had thus arrived at the mainstream stance that would mark the conservative movement to the present. Chamberlin once formulated a concise definition of what he and his colleagues sought to defend: "Conservatism at all times and in all countries has stood for religion, patriotism, the integrity of the family and respect for private property as the four pillars of a sound and healthy society."

The Soviet Planned Economic Order; 1931; reprinted, New York, Arno, 1970; *Russia's Iron Age;* 1934; reprinted, New York, Arno, 1970; *Collectivism—False Utopia;* New York, Macmillan, 1937; *The Confessions of an Individualist;* New York, Macmillan, 1940; *Beyond Containment;* Chicago, Henry Regnery, 1950; *The Evolution of a Conservative;* Chicago, Henry Regnery, 1959; *America's Second Crusade;* 1950; reprinted, R. Myles, 1962; *The Russian Revolution, 1917-1921;* New York, Macmillan, 1965.

Whittaker Chambers (1901-1961)

The Hiss-Chambers case is a fading memory for older Americans, and an obscure episode in American history for younger generations, but for conservatives the trial reverberates with a significance deeper than the final verdict. Whittaker Chambers had become a Communist Party member in the 1930s, undertaking some minor tasks for his superiors, but his disillusionment grew and he left the Party. While working as a senior editor for *Time* magazine, Chambers publicly accused a man named Alger Hiss of having been a Communist Party member. Hiss was a successful and respected New Deal-era diplomat who had been an adviser at the Yalta Conference and was president of the Carnegie Endowment for International Peace when Chambers made his accusation. Hiss was eventually convicted on two counts of perjury. (See Allen Weinstein, *Perjury: The Hiss-Chambers Case,* [New York, Random House, 1979] for a definitive account.) The trial and its aftermath aroused fierce emotions and became socially divisive: liberals in general treated Chambers as a deluded or malicious neurotic, and Hiss received their outpourings of sympathy, while conservatives banded together to defend Chambers from such self-serving caricatures. In *Witness,* Chambers gave his view of the trial and its larger meaning. The crisis of the twentieth century, he believed, is ultimately a spiritual one: Communism stands for man's attempt to dominate the world like a god, and will stop at nothing in order to achieve its mission; against it stands Western civilization, decadent and no longer willing to believe in anything. Chambers thought he heard the death rattle of the West, for liberalism, with its secular dream of social reconstruction, merely represented Communist messianism on a smaller scale. Liberalism was simply incapable of standing in the way of its secret ally; that was why Chambers believed he had left the "winning" side in breaking with the Party. Conservatives by and large do not share Chambers's fatalism, but they admire in him what William F. Buckley, Jr. has called "the keenest human understanding, reflected in . . . numinous prose, baptized in tragedy."

Witness; 1952; reprinted, Chicago, Regnery/Gateway; *Cold Friday;* New York, Random House, 1964; William F. Buckley, Jr., ed., *Odyssey of a Friend;* New York, G.P. Putnam, 1970.

Frank Chodorov (1887-1966)

His name is little known, and his books seldom read, but Frank Chodorov's influence on the post-war conservative movement is incalculable. In the 1940s, Chodorov, who has been called the inheritor of the intellectual tradition of Thomas Jefferson, Henry Thoreau, Henry George, and Albert Jay Nock, began to write and promote a brand of antistatist libertarianism, focusing on isolationism in foreign policy, and an opposition to the growth of the bureaucratic, welfare state policy at home. Witty, uncompromising, and energetic, Chodorov produced a small journal called *analysis,* and later became editor of *The*

Freeman, when it was purchased by the Foundation for Economic Education. Convinced that the intellectual battle could only be won in the academy, Chodorov founded the Intercollegiate Society of Individualists (ISI). ISI's first president was William F. Buckley, Jr., who was encouraged and stimulated by Chodorov. His near anarchistic libertarianism caused him to clash with many conservatives, but he remained an integral part of the movement until his death. ISI later became the Intercollegiate Studies Institute.

One Is a Crowd: Reflections of an Individualist; New York, Devin-Adair, 1952; *The Income Tax: Root of All Evil;* New York, Devin-Adair, 1954; *The Rise and Fall of Society: An Essay on the Economic Forces That Underlie Social Institutions;* New York, Devin-Adair, 1959; *Out of Step: The Autobiography of an Individualist;* New York, Devin-Adair, 1962; *Fugitive Essays: Selected Writings of Frank Chodorov;* Indianapolis, IN, Liberty Press, 1980.

Donald Davidson (1893-1968)

Donald Davidson was one of the Southern Agrarians, whose collection of essays, *I'll Take My Stand: The South and the Agrarian Tradition,* published in 1930, was a deeply conservative attack not just on "industrialism," but on the liberal, secular, progressivist worldview. Davidson's defense of the South's traditional life, centering around family, church, farm, and folk customs, included an attack on the liberal relativism that left man a rootless creature without identity. Davidson, a professor of English at Vanderbilt University for many years, shared these convictions with some of the other Agrarians, like John Crowe Ransom, Allen Tate, and Andrew Lytle, and as a teacher he influenced the conservative author, Richard M. Weaver. The contribution of Southerners to modern conservatism is immense, and embraces not only social critique, but literary criticism, history, and sociology.

I'll Take My Stand: The South and the Agrarian Tradition, by Twelve Southerners; 1930; reprinted, Baton Rouge, LA, Louisiana State University Press, 1980; *The Attack on Leviathan;* 1938; reprinted, Gloucester, MA, Peter Smith; *Still Rebels, Still Yankees and Other Essays;* Baton Rouge, LA, Louisiana State University Press, 1972; *Southern Writers in the Modern World;* Athens, GA, University of Georgia Press, 1958.

John Dos Passos (1896-1970)

As a young novelist, John Dos Passos wrote political fiction that denounced the factory owners for oppressing workers; later, he wrote novels criticizing union bosses. The liberal estimate of Dos Passos is that he "declined" over the years, but his increasing conservatism was the product of deep thought and meditation about American history. In one of his essays, he wrote: "In modern bureaucratic societies intellectuals are becoming a dominant class through their furnishing the bossmen with the slogans and delusions by which they control the general public. The twentieth century may well end by being known as the century of the intellectual." Dos Passos was not the only American artist whose worldview was conservative: Thornton Wilder, Robert Frost, and T.S. Eliot possessed spiritual and political insights of a profoundly conservative nature.

Midcentury: A Contemporary Chronicle; Boston, Houghton Mifflin, 1960; *Occasions and Protests;* Chicago, Henry Regnery, 1964; *The Prospect Before Us;* 1950; reprinted, New York, Greenwood, 1973.

Max Eastman (1883-1969)

Journalist, poet, and political writer, Max Eastman was one of the many ex-Communists whose "conversion" led them to conservative positions. As a young man he admired, and wrote a biography of, Leon Trotsky, and he edited for a time the radical paper, *The New Masses*. Though his faith in Communism dwindled in the 1920s, he tried to rationalize the purges and famines by attributing them to Stalin's personality. When he realized that the failure was that of socialism itself, he broke with the Left and became an extreme libertarian. A militant atheist, Eastman resigned from the editorial board of *National Review* because of its religious positions. His belief that economic and political liberty are mutually dependent has long been a tenet of conservatism.

The End of Socialism in Russia; Boston, Little, Brown, 1937; *Marxism, Is It Science?;* New York, W.W. Norton, 1940; *Stalin's Russia and the Crisis of Socialism;* New York, W.W. Norton, 1940; *Reflections on the Failure of Socialism;* 1955; reprinted, New York, Greenwood Press, 1982; *Love and Revolution;* New York, Random House, 1964.

M. Stanton Evans (1934-)

A veteran conservative journalist, M. Stanton Evans attended Yale University not long after William F. Buckley, Jr. At 28, he became the youngest editor of a metropolitan newspaper in America when he joined the *Indianapolis News*. After serving as the president of the American Conservative Union, Evans founded the Education and Research Institute. One of ERI's major programs is the National Journalism Center, which trains students in journalistic skills. Evans writes a syndicated column, has been a commentator on the CBS radio *Spectrum* program, and has contributed to *National Review* and *Human Events* for over twenty five years.

Revolt on the Campus; 1961; reprinted, New York, Greenwood Press, 1979; *The Future of Conservatism;* New York: Holt, Rinehart and Winston, 1968; *The Liberal Establishment;* New York: Devin-Adair, 1965; *The Politics of Surrender;* New York, Devin-Adair, 1966.

Milton Friedman (1912-)

Nobel Prize-winning economist Milton Friedman has been one of the reasons why conservative, free market economic analysis has received attention and respect in recent years in both the academy and public policy circles. He has long been associated with the "Chicago" school of economics, named for the scholars at the University of Chicago who have developed a sophisticated defense of the free market. Friedman's impact was first felt when his *Capitalism and Freedom* appeared: it defended, with verve and skill, the classical liberal heritage of limited government, and it took one form of government intervention after another to task for incompetence and failing to achieve intended aims. One of Friedman's single most important ideas was his understanding of the causes of the Great Depression: it was not the inevitable "business cycle," with its boom and bust, but the actions of the Federal Reserve Board, which artificially prolonged and worsened a momentary contraction. Friedman and his fellow "monetarists" have emphasized the importance of monetary policy, and have advocated a fixed annual increase in the money supply as the best way to avoid inflation and curb the caprices of the Federal Reserve Board. As George Nash notes, Friedman's influence has been so wide because he has suggested a batch of concrete, workable programs, some of which have been implemented (such as the all-volunteer Army), and others which have pushed public policy in a new direction (such as educational vouchers, which continue to be proposed in Congress against heavy lobbying by the National Education Association). Not all free enterprise economists agree with Friedman and the Chicago school: the "Austrian" economists distrust the use of mathematical analysis, and want the gold standard to be reinstated, whereas Friedman has advocated floating monetary rates. But the Chicago school remains one of the main streams in the conservative economic community.

Capitalism and Freedom; Chicago, University of Chicago

Press, 1962; *Essays in Positive Economics;* Chicago, University of Chicago Press, 1953; with Anna Schwartz, *A Monetary History of the United States, 1867-1960;* Princeton, Princeton University Press, 1963; *Tax Limitation, Inflation, and the Role of Government;* Dallas, TX, Fisher Institute, 1979; with Rose Friedman, *Free to Choose: A Personal Statement;* New York, Harcourt Brace Jovanovich, 1980.

George Gilder (1939-)

George Gilder has become somewhat caricatured as a "supply-side" economics guru, but he is more of a wide-ranging social critic than an economist. As a young man Gilder was involved with the Ripon Society type of liberal Republicanism. Meditating on the problems of sexuality and welfare, and inspired by the studies of Daniel P. Moynihan that proved the deleterious effects of welfare (specifically Aid to Families with Dependent Children) on the black family, Gilder wrote a book called *Sexual Suicide.* Gilder's thesis, which outraged feminists (among others) is that women's liberation and the modern sexual ethos have taken men out of the long-term, stable relationship of monogamy, based on the woman's nurturing, future-oriented personality, the result being a rise in male violence and crime. According to Gilder, sex has become, more than ever, a short-run exploitation on the masculine model. Gilder went on to document his thesis in two books which dealt with the way welfare encourages black women to become single mothers. *Wealth and Poverty* is really just a further development of Gilder's thought. Using at times nearly mystical rhetoric, Gilder argues here that capitalism is based on altruistic giving, risk-taking with no assurance of return. The entrepreneur has to be sensitive to the needs of the public, and his creative activity is the driving force behind social progress. From this it is easy to see why Gilder and other supply-siders argue for tax cuts: by encouraging investment rather than tax shelters, men will be more productive and willing to take innovative risks.

Sexual Suicide; New York, Bantam, 1975; *Naked Nomads: Unmarried Men in America;* New York, Times Books, 1974; *Visible Man: A True Story of Post-Racist America;* New York, Basic Books, 1978; *Wealth and Poverty;* New York, Basic Books, 1981; *The Spirit of Enterprise;* New York, Simon & Schuster, 1984; *Men and Marriage,* (revised edition of *Sexual Suicide*); Gretna, LA: Pelican Publishing Co., 1986.

Nathan Glazer (1923-)

In 1955 Nathan Glazer joined several prominent liberal intellectuals in *The New American Right* in attributing to post-war conservatives "authoritarian personalities," which arose from "maladjustment" to the complexities of the modern world. In 1972 he was publishing in *National Review.* What had happened in between was, of course, the 1960s; Glazer and other anti-Communist liberals found themselves dissatisfied with large-scale efforts at social reconstruction. Issues such as "urban renewal," where independent scholars like Edward Banfield and Jane Jacobs had proven the human cost of utopian city planning, began to make skeptics of men like Glazer, Daniel Patrick Moynihan, and Norman Podhoretz, the "neoconservatives." Glazer's own studies of busing and "affirmative action" quota hiring programs have become standard conservative critiques. He is regularly published in *Commentary* and *The Public Interest.*

With Daniel P. Moynihan, *Beyond the Melting Pot;* Cambridge, MA, MIT Press, 1970; *Affirmative Discrimination;* New York, Basic Books, 1975; with William Gorham, eds., *The Urban Predicament;* Washington, DC, Urban Institute, 1976.

John Hallowell (1913-)

At a time when the political science profession seemed completely dominated by the ideology of positivism, which accepts the absolute distinction between "fact" and "value" and claims to be "value-free," John Hallowell begged to differ. By divorcing politics from ethics, liberal political scientists had reduced politics to arbitrary power, Hallowell argued. Worse than that, however, was the fact that positivism left people prey to totalitarian ideologies, since there was no moral basis from which to judge them. Hallowell's connection between liberalism and totalitarianism became an essential part of the conservative critique, but he also showed that the classical and Christian tradition was alive and fully able to sustain a sophisticated political theory. In *The Moral Foundations of Democracy,* Hallowell outlined the natural law position. The three points, summarized by George Nash, are: 1) "there exists a meaningful reality," "an orderly universe," independent of the knower; 2) man can, by the use of his reason, discern the nature of reality; and 3) "knowledge of what man should do in order to fulfill his human nature is embodied in what has traditionally been called 'the law of nature' or the 'moral law.' " John Hallowell has been part of the movement to regain the classical/Christian tradition, and has been one of the best interpreters of the work of Eric Voegelin, a political philosopher who has pioneered that restoration.

The Decline of Liberalism as an Ideology; reprinted, New York, Fertig, 1971; *The Moral Foundations of Democracy;* 1954; reprinted, Chicago, University of Chicago Press, 1973.

Jeffrey Hart (1930-)

Professor of English at Dartmouth College and Senior Editor at *National Review,* Jeffrey Hart has always mixed his careers as a scholar and as a conservative polemicist. He has written extensively on eighteenth century politics and literature—the age of Bolingbroke, Burke, and Johnson. In 1966 he published *The American Dissent,* an attempt to evaluate the efforts of the *National Review* intellectual circle in its first ten years of activity.

Vicount Bolingbroke: Tory Humanist; London, Routledge & Kegan Paul, 1965; *The American Dissent;* New York, Double-day, 1966; *When the Going Was Good: American Life in the Fifties;* New York, Crown, 1982.

Friedrich A. von Hayek (1899-)

Friedrich von Hayek's *The Road to Serfdom* was the opening salvo in the conservative attack on the West's slide toward collectivism. Present in this book are the concepts which Hayek has elaborated and refined throughout his distinguished career as an economic and political scientist (a career which brought him an unexpected, but richly deserved Nobel Prize in 1974). Hayek declared that the move toward central economic planning was the first step toward tyranny, since small-scale intervention into the marketplace would give way to whole-scale control, as "adjustments" had to be made; so, too, the argument from "social justice" could never be satisfied until a complete redistribution of incomes had been achieved. From a strictly economic viewpoint, Hayek asserted, a single authority is not competent to manage a diverse economy: the knowledge necessary cannot be comprehended even by the largest computer: the knowledge is communicated in the millions of exchanges which occur daily in human activity. The only guarantee of freedom, Hayek went on to demonstrate, is the Rule of Law; that is, a group of impersonal rules which bound men equally. The alternative can only be rule by personal commands, which become arbitrary and benefit only a few, and spell the end of liberty. Hayek's debts to classical liberalism, and to his immediate mentor, the "Austrian" economist, Ludwig von Mises, are manifest. But whereas Hayek once claimed that he could not be called a "conservative," he has in recent years argued for a respect for tradition, which keeps men aware of the hard-won achievement of liberty and curbs their pride in trying to "remake" the world. See John Gray, *Hayek on Liberty* (New York, Basil Blackwell, 1984).

The Road to Serfdom; Chicago, University of Chicago Press, 1944; *Individualism and Economic Order,* Chicago, University of Chicago Press, 1958; *The Constitution of Liberty;* Chicago, University of Chicago Press, 1960; *The Counter-Revolution of Science;* Indianapolis, IN, Liberty Press, 1980; *Law, Legislation and Liberty,* 3 vols.; Chicago, University of Chicago Press, 1977, 1979; *The Pure Theory of Capital;* Chicago, University of Chicago Press, 1975; ed., *Capitalism and the Historians;* Chicago, University of Chicago Press, 1963.

Henry Hazlitt (1894-)

It may be hard to believe, but there was a time when Henry Hazlitt, one of the ablest defenders of the free market in this century, wrote editorials for *The New York Times.* A versatile and lucid journalist, Hazlitt was among the economic thinkers who reacted early on to the growing movement for central economic planning that gained momentum during World War II. His primer, *Economics in One Lesson,* warned that the efforts to seek a short-run benefit by some intervention in the marketplace inevitably did not take the long-run effects on the *whole* economy into account, thus paving the way for future crises. Hazlitt was one of the senior editors on *The Freeman,* a conservative/libertarian journal which was later bought by the Foundation for Economic Education. Over the years, Hazlitt played a central role in the effort to refute—practically point by point—the economic ideas of John Maynard Keynes, and the decline in Keynes's reputation is in no small way due to Hazlitt's arguments.

Economics in One Lesson; New Rochelle, NY, Arlington House, 1979; *The Failure of the 'New Economics': An Analysis of the Keynesian Fallacies;* 1959; reprinted, New Rochelle, NY, Arlington House, 1974; *The Foundations of Morality;* Menlo Park, CA, Institute for Humane Studies, 1972; ed., *The Critics of Keynesian Economics;* 1960; reprinted, New Rochelle, NY, Arlington House, 1977.

Will Herberg (1909-1977)

Will Herberg traveled the well-worn path from a youth in the 1920s and 1930s as a Communist activist to conservatism in the post-war period. But Herberg's brilliance as a sociologist of religion and his spiritual sensitivity set him apart as one of the finest scholars of his generation. Calmly, persistently, and with a persuasiveness that emerged from rigorous thought, Herberg contended that the social and moral orders are not "relative," open to reconstruction by social planners or utopian crusaders, but tied to certain metaphysical and enduring truths which we discard at our peril. Herberg's *Protestant Catholic Jew* is widely considered the most comprehensive study of American religion ever written. For many years he was the religion editor of *National Review.* Soon after Herberg's death, a special issue of *National Review* (August 5, 1977) was devoted to assessing his achievement.

Protestant Catholic Jew; Garden City, NY, Doubleday, 1955; *Judaism and Modern Man;* New York, Atheneum, 1970; ed., *Four Existentialist Theologians;* 1958; reprinted, New York, Greenwood Press, 1975.

Harry Jaffa (1918-)

Professor of political science at Claremont McKenna College, Harry Jaffa is one of the leading students of the political philosopher, Leo Strauss. Jaffa's conservatism has raised many controversies in conservative circles because he holds that the doctrine of equality, as embodied in the Declaration of Independence, is the norm for American politics. This had led him to an admiration for Abraham Lincoln, a figure many conservatives regard as a utopian and an architect of a powerful, centralized government. Aside from his many scholarly achievements, Jaffa can claim credit as the author of Barry Goldwater's famous remark: "Extremism in the defense of liberty is no vice, moderation in the pursuit of justice is no virtue."

Thomism and Aristotelianism; 1952; reprinted, New York, Greenwood Press, 1979; *Crisis of the House Divided;* 1959; reissued, with a new preface, Chicago, University of Chicago Press, 1982; with Allan Bloom, *Shakespeare's Politics;* New York, Basic Books, 1965; *The Conditions of Freedom: Essays in Political Philosophy;* Baltimore, Johns Hopkins University Press, 1975.

Willmoore Kendall (1909-1967)

Despite the fact that Willmoore Kendall collaborated on most of his books and essays, and engaged in perpetual debates and fallings-out with conservative writers, his personality and distinctive thought have always come through loud and clear, and he is regularly acknowledged to be one of the central conservative thinkers of the post-war period. In contrast to writers who have tried to place conservatism in a European context, Kendall asserted that America's political tradition was unique and that American conservatives were preserving the system created by the Founding Fathers and defended in *The Federalist*. A continuing theme in Kendall's writings is that far from an "open" or "pluralist" society, American politics is based on the "deliberate sense of the community," or a "consensus society," mediated by the virtuous statesmen of the legislative assemblies. His experience as a Trotskyite sympathizer during the 1930s convinced him that liberalism was ill-equipped to make distinctions and definitions, and that without such judgments, anarchy and, eventually, tyranny would be the result. This perspective allowed him to comment on such phenomena as the McCarthy era and the "Imperial" presidency with an unrivalled trenchancy. As a teacher, he influenced William F. Buckley, Jr., L. Brent Bozell, Garry Wills, and others.

With Austin Ranney, *Democracy and the American Party System;* 1956; reprinted, New York, Greenwood Press, 1975; *John Locke and the Doctrine of Majority Rule;* Urbana, IL, University of Illinois Press, 1965; *The Conservative Affirmation;* 1963; reprinted, Chicago, Henry Regnery, 1985; with George W. Carey, *The Basic Symbols of the American Political Tradition;* Baton Rouge, LA, Louisiana State University Press, 1970; *Contra Mundum;* New Rochelle, NY, Arlington House, 1971.

Hugh Kenner (1923-)

Hugh Kenner's work does not strictly fit into a conservative/liberal framework, since he is primarily a literary critic. But as one of the outstanding authorities on the modernist writers—James Joyce, T.S. Eliot, Ezra Pound, Wyndham Lewis—Kenner has been sensitive to their conservative political and philosophical ideas. He has also occasionally demolished attempts to call these writers "fascists." Kenner has written for *National Review.*

Paradox in Chesterton; New York, Sheed & Ward, 1947; *Wyndham Lewis;* New York, New Directions, 1954; *The Invisible Poet: T.S. Eliot;* New York, McDowell, Oblensky, 1959; *The Pound Era;* Berkeley, University of California Press, 1971.

James Jackson Kilpatrick (1920-)

Known to the TV age as the feisty conservative opponent of Shana Alexander on the old Point/Counterpoint segment of *60 Minutes,* James Kilpatrick is a nationally syndicated columnist whose prose style is even more rewarding than his screen appearances. In 1957, as the young editor of the *Richmond News Leader,* Kilpatrick published a book entitled, *The Sovereign States,* a blistering attack on the *Brown v. Board of Education* Supreme Court decision mandating school integration. Kilpatrick argued that the decision was a palpable encroachment on states' rights by a branch of the federal government, a dangerous curtailing of freedom and sovereignty. Though his Southern background lay behind his attack, conservatives in general concurred with Kilpatrick's assessment of the centrality of federalism to American politics, and he has continued to write on the subject for *National Review* and in his column.

The Sovereign States; Chicago, Henry Regnery, 1957; *The Smut Peddlers;* 1960; reprinted, New York, Greenwood Press, 1973; with Eugene McCarthy, *A Political Bestiary;* New York, Avon, 1979.

Russell Kirk (1918-)

Russell Kirk is one of the Founding Fathers of modern American conservatism. *The Conservative Mind,* published in 1953, provided conservatives with an intellectual patrimony, a continuous tradition of brilliant thinkers applying conservative principles to their times. Kirk looked to Edmund Burke as the founder of conservatism: Burke's appreciation of the common law, embedded in the institutions which grew up over the centuries, made him acutely aware of the dangers of Enlightenment ideologues who believed they could remake society. The handiwork of those ideologues was the French Revolution, and it has continued to the present to pose a fundamental challenge to the Western nations. Kirk believed that Burke was all too "relevant" to contemporary America. Kirk's distrust of "rationalism in politics" and his ranking of "order" over "freedom" as the first need of society has drawn fire from various sources, but he has never been a proponent of irrationalism. Rather, he argues that the valid traditional institutions of Western culture still remain intact, if badly weakened, and that the imaginative leadership of virtuous statesmen is needed to effect prudent change. The author of over 20 books, including fiction, literary criticism, and several books on education, Kirk founded *Modern Age* and has been a contributor to *National Review* from its inception.

John Randolph of Roanoke; 1951; reprinted, Indianapolis, IN, Liberty Press, 1978; *The Conservative Mind: From Burke to Eliot;* 1953; seventh rev. ed., Chicago, Henry Regnery, 1986; *The American Cause;* 1957; reprinted, New York, Greenwood Press, 1975; *Confessions of a Bohemian Tory;* New York, Fleet, 1963; *Edmund Burke: A Genius Reconsidered;* New Rochelle, NY, Arlington House, 1967; *Enemies of the Permanent Things;* 1969; reprinted, La Salle, IL, Sherwood Sugden, 1984; *The Roots of American Order;* Pepperdine, CA, Pepperdine University Press, 1974; *Eliot and His Age;* 1971; reprinted, La Salle, IL, Sherwood Sugden, 1984; *Decadence and Renewal in the Higher Learning;* Chicago, Regnery/Gateway, 1978; ed., *The Portable Conservative Reader;* New York, Viking, 1983.

Irving Kristol (1920-)

Along with Nathan Glazer and Norman Podhoretz, Irving Kristol is a central figure in the neoconservative movement. A Trotskyist as a young man, Kristol had become a "cold war liberal" by the 1950s, though far from an admirer of conservatism. The social upheaval of the 1960s acted as a catalyst for Kristol and others, and the neoconservatives found themselves taking a "conservative" position on economic and social issues, such as pornography, quota hiring policies, and welfare reform. In 1966 he founded *The Public Interest* with sociologist Daniel Bell, and it quickly became an influential forum for neoconservative policy analysis. While many of the neoconservatives tend to concentrate on social policy alone, Kristol has written widely about the moral and philosophical underpinnings of the American political tradition, and has acknowledged his debt to the philosopher, Leo Strauss.

On the Democratic Idea in America; New York, Harper &

Row, 1972; *Two Cheers for Capitalism;* New York, Basic Books, 1978; *Reflections of a Neoconservative: Looking Back, Looking Ahead;* New York, Basic Books, 1983.

Eugene Lyons (1898-1985)

Like his English counterpart, Malcolm Muggeridge, Eugene Lyons went to the Soviet Union on a journalistic assignment, full of utopian hopes for the worker's paradise. (As a young leftist he had written a defense of Sacco and Vanzetti.) After witnessing the self-inflicted famines and purges, Lyons, like Muggeridge, became bitterly disillusioned—especially at the gullibility and complicity of liberal intellectuals. He coined the term, "the Red Decade" for the 1930s, and it became the title of his book indicting Western liberalism. Lyons wrote several other penetrating books on the Soviet Union.

The Red Decade; 1941; reprinted, New Rochelle, NY, Arlington House, 1971; *Assignment in Utopia;* New York, Harcourt, Brace, and World, 1937; *Moscow Carousel;* New York, Knopf, 1935.

Frank Meyer (1909-1972)

For contemporary conservatives, who take many of their principles for granted, it may seem hard to understand all the furor in the 1950s and early 1960s that took place among conservative polemicists over the primacy of "freedom" or "order," and the place of the individual in society. Frank Meyer, a founding editor of *National Review,* and conservative polemicist, argued vigorously for "fusionism," an integration of libertarianism, with its emphasis on the primacy of individual freedom, and traditionalism, with its belief in order and virtue as the bedrock of society. The volume he edited, *What is Conservatism?,* was an attempt to bring the sides together. Meyer's *In Defense of Freedom* sided substantially with the libertarians, though he conceded that freedom only had meaning within the context of Judeo-Christian principles. The ensuing debate over the book did in fact cause conservatives to treat both sides seriously. For instance, Russell Kirk, who disagreed vociferously with Meyer, later titled a chapter in his book, *The Roots of American Order,* "The Tension Between Freedom and Order." As a young man, Meyer was a committed Communist Party member, and when he rejected Communism, he became equally tireless in opposition. Though he left behind no single, great book, his regular column in *National Review,* "Principles and Heresies," was constantly stimulating and incisive.

The Moulding of Communists; New York, Harcourt, Brace and World, 1961; *In Defense of Freedom;* Chicago, Henry Regnery, 1962; ed., *What is Conservatism?;* New York, Holt, Rinehart and Winston, 1954; *The Conservative Mainstream;* New Rochelle, NY, Arlington House, 1969.

Ludwig von Mises (1881-1973)

Ludwig von Mises has been overshadowed in reputation by his student, the Nobel Prize-winning economist, Friedrich von Hayek. But Mises was the other major proponent of the "Austrian" school of economic thought. The central tenet of this school is embodied in the title of Mises's *magnum opus: Human Action.* The "Austrians" hold that an economy is not a machine, with predictable moving parts, but a myriad of individuals making choices and valuations. No centralized bureaucracy can have the knowledge which is exchanged daily by market participants in millions of individual transactions. Mises lived during the heyday of Keynesian economics, but his ideas have influenced several generations of younger scholars and, notably, the "supply side" theorists, who concentrate on the choices individuals make when confronting entrepreneurial risk-taking. A firm proponent of the gold standard and a stable money supply, Mises may yet prove a prophetic figure.

Bureaucracy; 1944; reprinted, Cedar Falls, IA, Center for Futures Education, 1983; *Human Action: A Treatise on Economics;* 1944; 3rd rev. ed., Chicago, Henry Regnery, 1966; *Socialism;* 1951; reprinted, Indianapolis, IN, Liberty Press, 1981; *The Anti-Capitalist Mentality;* 1956; reprinted, New York, Libertarian Press, 1978; *Planned Chaos;* Irvington-on-Hudson, NY, Foundation for Economic Education, 1961; *The Theory of Money and Credit;* Irvington-on-Hudson, NY, Foundation for Economic Education, 1971; *A Critique of Interventionism;* New Rochelle, NY, Arlington House, 1977.

Thomas Molnar (1921-)

Born in Hungary, Thomas Molnar, Catholic historian and political scientist, survived the Nazi concentration camp at Dachau, only to confront the tightening grip of the Soviet Union on his native country. Escaping to Belgium, Molnar eventually emigrated to the United States. His developing critique of utopianism is anchored to a traditionalist, Thomistic worldview. Molnar's arguments against egalitarianism and "pluralism," especially in their American incarnation, have long been a part of the conservative analysis of contemporary society. Always in touch with the intellectual climate in Europe, Molnar has been a frequent contributor to *National Review, The Intercollegiate Review,* and other journals.

The Future of Education; 1961; reprinted, New York, Fleet, 1970; *The Decline of the Intellectual;* 1962; reprinted, New Rochelle, NY, Arlington House, 1973; *Utopia: The Perennial Heresy;* New York, Sheed & Ward, 1967; *Sartre, Ideologue of Our Time;* New York, Sheed & Ward, 1968; *The Counter-Revolution;* New York, Funk & Wagnalls, 1969; *God and the Knowledge of Reality;* New York, Basic Books, 1974; *Authority and Its Enemies;* New Rochelle, NY, Arlington House, 1976; *Christian Humanism: A Critique of the Secular City & Its Ideology;* Chicago, Franciscan Herald Press, 1978; *Theists and Atheists: A Typology of Non-Belief;* Mouton, France, 1979.

Felix Morley (1891-1982)

More of an old-style classical liberal than conservative, Felix Morley was a journalist, President of Haverford College, and co-founder of *Human Events.* His Quaker background led to an isolationist, no-foreign-entanglements position, causing him to resign from *Human Events,* which took a more "internationalist" stance—a common difference between conservatives in the 1940s and early 1950s. Profoundly antagonistic to Franklin Delano Roosevelt's willingness to alter the balance of powers in American government in the cause of "democracy," Morley wrote *Freedom and Federalism* to defend the handiwork of the Founding Fathers.

The Power in the People; 1949; reprinted, Menlo Park, CA, Institute for Humane Studies, 1972; *Freedom and Federalism;* Chicago, Henry Regnery, 1959; *For the Record;* Chicago, Henry Regnery, 1979; *Essays on Individuality;* Indianapolis, IN, Liberty Press, 1977.

John Courtney Murray, S.J. (1904-1967)

One of the ongoing debates in American history and political thought has been the question: to what extent is America the creation of Enlightenment and Lockean principles? Was its Founding a modern, rationalist experiment? Most conservatives have answered in the negative, and John Courtney Murray's *We Hold These Truths* buttressed their arguments by placing America in a continuous European tradition undergirded by the concept of natural law. In so doing, Murray was showing not only that Roman Catholics can be reconciled to the American political order, but also that the notion that America's is a "liberal" tradition of social experiment and "change" is erroneous. Willmoore Kendall called the book "a major breakthrough in American political *science.*"

Morality and Modern War; New York, Church Peace Union, 1959; *We Hold These Truths;* New York, Doubleday Image, 1964; *The Problem of God: Yesterday and Today;* New Haven, CT, Yale University Press, 1964; *The Problem of Religious Freedom;* Westminster, MD, Newman Press, 1965.

Gerhart Niemeyer (1907-)

As a young man in Germany, Gerhart Niemeyer was an ardent socialist, and his criticisms of the Nazis—from the Left—forced him to emigrate. Later, as a professor in America, he came to realize the threat of totalitarian ideologies, and the impotence of liberalism to deal with that threat. He settled at Notre Dame, and wrote a number of analyses of Communism, demonstrating that Marxist-Leninist theory was in fact the only adequate guide to Soviet practice. For a time he worked for the State Department and the Council on Foreign Relations, and for many years he contributed a regular column, "Days and Works," to *National Review.* But beyond his studies of Communism, Niemeyer has contributed significantly in the area of political philosophy, and is one of the foremost interpreters of the philosophy of Eric Voegelin.

Law Without Force; Princeton, Princeton University Press, 1941; *An Inquiry Into the Soviet Mentality;* New York, Praeger, 1956; *Facts on Communism: The Communist Ideology;* Washington, DC, Government Printing Office, 1959; *Deceitful Peace;* New Rochelle, NY, Arlington House, 1971; *Between Nothingness and Paradise;* Baton Rouge, LA, Louisiana State University Press, 1971; *Aftersight and Foresight: Selected Essays;* Lanham, MD, University Press of America/ Intercollegiate Studies Institute, 1987 (forthcoming).

Robert Nisbet (1913-)

An erudite and urbane sociologist, Robert Nisbet has, in many ways, taken Alexis de Tocqueville as his model. Like Tocqueville, Nisbet has been sensitive to the mores and institutions which have preserved liberty in the American democracy. His belief is that the "intermediate institutions"— family, church, club, union, and the like—have been weakened by the growth of a paternalistic government, and that there is less of a protective buffer between the individual and the state. The loss of community and of authority are constant themes in Nisbet's writings. Needless to say, Nisbet's views are far from common in the sociological profession, but he brilliantly shows how many of the nineteenth-century sociologists confirm his insights.

The Quest for Community; New York, Oxford University Press, 1962; *The Sociological Tradition;* New York, Basic Books, 1967; *Social Change and History;* New York, Oxford University Press, 1969; *The Social Bond,* with Robert G. Perrin; New York, Knopf, 1977; *The Degradation of the Academic Dogma;* New York, Basic Books, 1971; *The Twilight of Authority;* New York, Oxford University Press, 1975; *History of the Idea of Progress;* New York, Basic Books, 1979; *Prejudices: A Philosophical Dictionary;* Cambridge, MA, Harvard University Press, 1982.

Norman Podhoretz (1930-)

Presiding over *Commentary* magazine, the forum of the neoconservatives, Norman Podhoretz represents a significant change in the American cultural landscape. The genesis of the neoconservative movement was the reaction of those in the Jewish intellectual community who had become anti-Communists to those who remained sympathetic, or at least uncritical, toward the Soviet Union. But it reached a turning point when the neoconservatives began to attack liberal social policies as counterproductive and misguided. Podhoretz has been responsible for publishing many of these critiques, though his own interests have been dominated by the need for American military and diplomatic strength in response to the Soviet threat.

Making It; New York, Harper & Row, 1980; *Breaking Ranks: A Political Memoir;* New York, Harper & Row, 1980; *The Present Danger;* New York, Simon & Schuster, 1980; *Why We Were in Vietnam;* New York, Simon & Schuster, 1982; *The Bloody Crossroads: Where Literature and Politics Meet;* New York, Simon and Schuster, 1986.

Leonard Read (1898-1983)

Leonard Read began his career as a businessman, but he was really an evangelist—for the free market, private property system, as he called it. He founded the Foundation for Economic Education (FEE) in the late 1940s, and built it into an effective educational organization, sponsoring dozens of seminars, publishing books and a journal, *The Freeman,* and promoting the research and writing of its staff members. Never a highbrow organization, Read made FEE speak simply and clearly to businessmen, school teachers, and college students.

Henry Regnery (1912-)

It is hard to imagine how the conservative movement could have had such an impact on American culture without the existence of the Henry Regnery Company, so integral has this publisher been to the national intellectual debate. Beginning in 1947, and continuing to the present, Henry Regnery has brought the finest conservative books, from economics and foreign policy to aesthetics and theology, before the public. The authors he has published include not only conservative writers like Russell Kirk, James Burnham, Frank Meyer, William F. Buckley, Jr., and Whittaker Chambers, but poets, novelists, and statesmen, like Ezra Pound, Wyndham Lewis, Konrad

Adenauer, and John Dos Passos. Walking on thin financial ice for nearly forty years, Henry Regnery has maintained the most cultured, urbane, and principled conservative press in America.

Memoirs of a Dissident Publisher; New York, Harcourt, Brace, Jovanovich, 1979.

Wilhelm Roepke (1899-1966)

Though he never lived in America, Wilhelm Roepke, a German economist, became influential in the developing conservative defense of the free market economy. Roepke was a chief advisor to Ludwig Erhardt, who launched Germany's post-war "economic miracle" by a policy of deregulation. Unlike many of the "Austrian" and "monetarist" economists, whose ideas about human nature and government are shallow, and influenced primarily by abstract individualism, Roepke was a man of broad culture, basing his ideas on religious concepts. He believed that a free society could only exist if supported by a virtuous people: "Self-discipline, a sense of justice, honesty, fairness, chivalry, moderation, public spirit, respect for human dignity, firm ethical norms—all of these are things which people must possess before they go to market to compete with each other."

The Economics of a Free Society; Chicago, Henry Regnery, 1963; *Against the Tide;* Chicago, Henry Regnery, 1969; *A Humane Economy;* Chicago, Henry Regnery, 1960.

Murray Rothbard (1926-)

As the conservative movement grew in the post-war years, it consisted of a loose coalition of groups which shared common goals, including a rejection of the paternalistic state and government intervention into the marketplace. The "libertarians" were and are largely inheritors of the classical liberal tradition of extreme individualism and laissez-faire economics, which they have combined with the American tradition of isolationism. They often describe their position as "anarchist," favoring private police, judicial, and defense functions, in addition to more common policies, such as legalization of marijuana and the abolition of "victimless crimes." Murray Rothbard, a student of Ludwig von Mises and proponent of the "Austrian" school of economics, has been one of the libertarians' intellectual leaders. According to George Nash, Rothbard believes that the Right was taken over by doctrinaire anti-Communists and emigré Catholics. Libertarianism has gone its separate way by and large, even to the extent of forming a political party, and Rothbard continues as one of its principal spokesmen.

For a New Liberty: The Libertarian Manifesto; New York, Macmillan, 1978; *America's Great Depression;* New York, New York University Press, 1975; *The Ethics of Liberty;* New York, Humanities Press, 1982; *Man, Economy & State,* 2 volumes; New York, New York University Press, 1979.

William Rusher (1923-)

The Publisher of *National Review* began his political career as a quintessentially "moderate" Republican, but the liberal hysteria over Senator McCarthy disturbed him and drove him to seek a more principled position. Rusher was an integral part of the "draft Goldwater" group, and continued as an advisor. As the Republican Party continued to drift in the 1960s and 1970s, Rusher hoped that a conservative third party could be founded, a party that would draw disaffected Democrats as well as conservative Republicans. Known as a skillful debater (and an author of a book on the subject), Rusher regularly appeared on the television program, *The Advocates.* He writes a syndicated column, "The Conservative Advocate."

The Making of the New Majority Party; Ottawa, IL, Green

175

Hill, 1975; *How to Win Arguments;* New York, Doubleday, 1981; *The Rise of the Right;* New York, Morrow, 1984.

William Schlamm (1904-1978)

A Jewish emigré from Austria, where he had become an outspoken critic of Hitler and Stalin, William Schlamm became an editor of *Fortune* magazine, and an advisor to Henry Luce. After leaving the *Time* empire, Schlamm worked on *The Freeman,* which was then racked with internal disputes. In 1952 he met William F. Buckley, Jr., and along with James Burnham became one of the founders of *National Review.* Though he engaged in heated debates with NR's editors, and eventually returned to Europe, his articulate anti-Communism helped to shape the journal's editorial thrust.

Leo Strauss (1899-1973)

If the test of an outstanding teacher is the number of brilliant students he generates, then Leo Strauss is one of the most influential teachers of this or any other century; it is said that the "Straussians" now are the single largest group within the American Political Science Association. Like Eric Voegelin, Strauss rejected positivism and historicism, and rehabilitated the practice of political *philosophy.* His close, interpretive readings of the classical texts paralleled the movement in literary criticism known as the New Criticism. For Strauss, the nature of modernity is characterized by a rejection of natural law, by which men could order themselves and society, in favor of a theory of natural "rights" based on the need to control man's "passions." Hobbes, for example, based the motive for the social contract on the fear of death. Though Strauss studied the major writers from Plato and Aristotle through Machiavelli, Hobbes, and Rousseau, his analysis shed light on modern totalitarian ideologies, and helped to form the conservative critique of liberalism.

On Tyranny, revised & enlarged edition; Ithaca, NY, Cornell University Press, 1968; *Natural Right and History;* Chicago, University of Chicago Press, 1965; *What is Political Philosophy?;* 1959; reprinted, New York, Greenwood Press, 1973; *History of Political Philosophy,* with Joseph Cropsey, eds.; Chicago, University of Chicago Press, 1981; *The Political Philosophy of Hobbes;* Chicago, University of Chicago Press, 1963; *The City and Man;* Chicago, University of Chicago Press, 1978; *Liberalism, Ancient and Modern;* New York, Basic Books, 1968; *Thoughts on Machiavelli;* Chicago, University of Chicago Press, 1978.

Ralph de Toledano (1916-)

Like many of the most passionate of the post-war conservatives, Ralph de Toledano was a convert from the prevailing liberal climate of the 1930s, brought "over" by the "show trials" of Stalin and the Stalin-Hitler pact. With another anti-communist activist, Isaac Don Levine, he founded *Plain Talk,* a journal which later merged with *The Freeman.* Toledano covered the Hiss-Chambers case for *Newsweek* and, according to George Nash, he began the assignment still a "man of the Left." But the self-serving behavior of several liberals at the trial left him disillusioned, and he became a close friend of Whittaker Chambers. *Seeds of Treason,* written with Victor Lasky, is Toledano's evaluation of the trial. Toledano's willingness to take on powerful spokesmen of the Left—including, recently, Ralph Nader—has in several instances cost him personally. In addition to his role as social commentator, Toledano is an accomplished poet and jazz critic, and still contributes regularly to *National Review.*

Seeds of Treason: The True Story of the Hiss-Chambers Tragedy, with Victor Lasky; 1950; reprinted, Chicago, Henry Regnery, 1962; *Lament for a Generation;* New York, Farrar, Straus, Giroux, 1960.

Stephen Tonsor (1923-)

Professor of History at the University of Michigan and Associate Editor of *Modern Age,* Stephen Tonsor has been for many years a major contributor to the conservative intellectual discussion. His independence from any form of "party line" is notable; he has, for instance, argued against Edmund Burke's relevance for the American political tradition, and he has defended large universities against the conservative preference for small, private colleges. He is currently working on a major study of the history of the idea of "equality."

Tradition and Reform in American Education; La Salle, IL, Open Court, 1974.

Freda Utley (1898-1978)

Freda Utley was one of the many conservatives whose intellectual pilgrimage was aided by raw experience. The daughter of a Fabian socialist, Utley embraced Communism and married a Russian named Arcadia Berdichevsky and emigrated to the Soviet Union. Her disenchantment there came swiftly, and it was destined to be complete. Her husband was arrested, tried, and eventually "disappeared." *The Dream We Lost* tells her story. She went on to a career as a foreign policy commentator, writing books on the rise of Communism in China, the Middle East, and Asia. Henry Regnery has called her "a shrewd, tireless observer" with "a fine mind, enormous vitality, and, above all, a strong sense of justice...."

Lost Illusion (also titled *The Dream We Lost: Soviet Russia Then and Now*); New York, John Day, 1940; *Last Chance in China;* Indianapolis, IN, Bobbs-Merrill, 1947; *The High Cost of Vengeance;* Chicago, Henry Regnery, 1949; *The China Story;* Chicago, Henry Regnery, 1951; *Odyssey of a Liberal: Memoirs;* Washington, DC, Washington National Press, 1970.

Ernest van den Haag (1914-)

Sociologist and professor of law at Fordham University, Ernest van den Haag emigrated from Mussolini's Italy. A tough-minded critic who does not embrace religiously based conservatism, van den Haag is a supreme example of a scholar who uses the tools of social science to dismantle liberal public policy. He has been a leading defender of capital punishment, and a relentless critic of court-mandated integration, the minimum wage, and the welfare state.

Passion and Social Constraint; New York, Stein & Day, 1963; *Punishing Criminals;* New York, Basic Books, 1975; *Capitalism: Sources of Hostility,* ed.; Washington, DC, Heritage Foundation, 1979; with John P. Conrad, *The Death Penalty;* New York, Plenum, 1983.

Peter Viereck (1916-)

Though he has been accused of being an impostor and a closet liberal, Peter Viereck played an important and enduring role in establishing conservatism as a respectable political tradition during and after World War II. Like Russell Kirk, Viereck's conservatism embraced the European tradition; similar to Kirk too was his effort at demonstrating a formidable intellectual tradition, "from John Adams to Churchill." Viereck loathed the Stalinist fellow-traveling intellectuals of the 1930s, the elitist champions of the Common Man, and he joined James Burnham and other conservatives in going beyond "containment" by calling for a rollback of Communist frontiers. But Viereck was also violently anti-capitalist, seeing "Manchester economics" as vulgar and materialistic, and his heroes included such "conservative socialists" as Metternich and Disraeli (in this he has affinities with a contemporary conservative commentator—George Will). During the peak of the McCarthy hysteria, Viereck condemned conservatives for any support of the Senator, and he became permanently estranged from mainstream conservative circles.

Conservatism Revisited: The Revolt Against Revolt, 1815-1949, with the addition of 'The New Conservatism—What Went Wrong?'; 1962; reprinted, New York, Greenwood Press, 1978; *Conservatism: From John Adams to Churchill;* 1956; reprinted, New York, Greenwood Press, 1978; *Shame and Glory of the Intellectuals;* 1953; reprinted, New York, Greenwood Press, 1978.

Eliseo Vivas (1901-)

Born in Venezuela, Eliseo Vivas emigrated to the United States as a young man and in his early career he became an adherent of the reigning school of "naturalism" in philosophy, presided over by John Dewey. After a period of intense questioning and thought, precipitated by the horrible events surrounding World War II, Vivas concluded that naturalism did not adequately explain human nature, and that it excluded the realm of objective value. *The Moral Life and the Ethical Life,* a thorough critique of naturalism, was the result of his inner struggles. In his subsequent career, Vivas also wrote extensively on aesthetics, a field to which modern conservatives have rarely contributed. A professor at the University of Chicago and Northwestern University, Vivas has long been an advisor to *Modern Age* and *The Intercollegiate Review.* See *Viva Vivas! Essays in Honor of Eliseo Vivas;* Indianapolis, IN, Liberty Press, 1976, and Hugh Curtler, *A Theory of Art, Tragedy and Culture;* New York, Haven Publishing Corp., 1981.

The Moral Life and the Ethical Life; Chicago, University of Chicago Press, 1950; *Creation and Discovery: Essays in Criticism and Aesthetics;* Chicago, Regnery/Gateway, 1966; *D.H. Lawrence: The Failure and the Triumph of Art;* Bloomington,

IN, Indiana University Press, 1964; *Contra Marcuse;* New Rochelle, NY, Arlington House, 1971; *Two Roads to Ignorance: A QuasiBiography;* Carbondale, IL, Southern Illinois University Press, 1979.

Eric Voegelin (1901-1985)

Modern conservatives have often defined themselves as opponents of "ideology," meaning by that term a closed system of abstract ideas which seeks power over human society. Eric Voegelin is perhaps the philosopher in this century who did more than any other to diagnose the cancer of ideology and to restore the practice of philosophy in its classical and Christian fulness. Voegelin is known for his likening of modern ideology to "gnosticism," a heretical sect that believed the world was evil and claimed that it was privy to the secret knowledge (*gnosis*) of how to achieve goodness. In the same sense, Marxism, for example, claims to have the *gnosis* of the "laws of history," and that the currently evil capitalist dispensation must be completely supplanted by socialism. In his classic work, *The New Science of Politics,* Voegelin showed the inadequacy of positivistic political science, and traced the rise of modern gnosticism. A scholar of immense erudition, Voegelin's *magnum opus* is his five-volume work, *Order and History,* in which he sought "to derive the 'order of history' from the 'history of order.' " Though he came to believe that there is no pattern or "meaning" in history that can definitively be known by man, he believed history to be a record of the spiritual drama of mankind. See Ellis Sandoz, *The Voegelinian Revolution: A Biographical Introduction;* Baton Rouge, LA, Louisiana State University Press, 1981.

The New Science of Politics; Chicago, University of Chicago Press, 1952; *Science, Politics and Gnosticism;* Chicago, Regnery/Gateway, 1968; *From Enlightenment to Revolution;*

Durham, NC, Duke University Press, 1975; *Order and History,* five volumes, *Israel and Revelation, The World of the Polis, Plato and Aristotle, The Ecumenic Age* and *In Search of Order* (forthcoming); Baton Rouge, LA, Louisiana State University Press, 1956, 1957, 1971.

Richard M. Weaver (1910-1963)

Richard Weaver's role in modern conservative thought is central, and his *Ideas Have Consequences* is one of its major documents. In that book he argued that the split which came between man's knowledge of transcendent reality and his categories of thought, beginning with the medieval "nominalists," had left the modern world without moral norms, and hence prey to ideologies which claimed a monopoly on truth. Weaver's critique of liberalism, which is egalitarian and relativistic, was uncompromising; civilization, he said, was based on "distinction and hierarchy." Though he did not emphasize it publicly, Weaver's background as a Southerner deeply influenced his thought, especially in his belief in the importance of morally-grounded rhetoric. Though conservatives have disagreed with some of Weaver's pronouncements, he remains a seminal thinker who continues to be read.

Ideas Have Consequences; Chicago, University Press, 1948; *The Ethics of Rhetoric;* Chicago, Regnery/Gateway, 1965; *Visions of Order;* Baton Rouge, Louisiana State University Press, 1964; *Life Without Prejudice and other Essays;* Chicago, Henry Regnery, 1965; *The Southern Tradition at Bay;* New Rochelle, NY, Arlington House, 1968.

Frederick Wilhelmsen (1923-)

A conservative Roman Catholic who early became a champion of "traditionalism," Wilhelmsen has been part of the movement to effect a restoration of classical and medieval political philosophy. He was associated with the short-lived, conservative Catholic magazine, *Triumph,* and has taught for many years at the University of Dallas.

Hilaire Belloc: No Alienated Man; New York, Sheed & Ward, 1953; *The Metaphysics of Love;* New York, Sheed & Ward, 1962; *Christianity and Political Philosophy;* Athens, GA, University of Georgia Press, 1978; *Citizen of Rome: Reflections from the Life of a Roman Catholic;* La Salle, IL, Sherwood Sugden, 1980.

George Will (1941-)

With a syndicated column appearing in 380 newspapers around the country, and regular appearances as a political commentator for ABC News, George Will may be the most influential conservative journalist in America. Will's clarity of style and firm principles earned him this prominence—and the 1977 Pulitzer Prize for commentary. "A lapsed professor of political science" (as he calls himself), Will was *National Review*'s Washington editor from 1973-1975. Will's conservatism has always differed significantly from the mainstream: his model statesman is Benjamin Disraeli, who combined Tory nationalism with the beginning of the welfare state in Britain. In *Statecraft as Soulcraft*, Will generated controversy in conservative circles by claiming that the welfare state was necessary and even capable of cultivating the good society. Though most conservatives see the welfare state as inimical to virtue, Will's Aristotelian emphasis on the role of government in inculcating character in its citizens reflects one strain of modern conservatism.

The Pursuit of Happiness and Other Sobering Thoughts; New York, Harper & Row, 1978; *The Pursuit of Virtue and Other*

Tory Notions; New York, Simon & Schuster, 1982; *Statecraft as Soulcraft: What Government Does;* New York, Simon & Schuster, 1983.

Francis G. Wilson (1901-1976)

In the period immediately after World War II, several major thinkers were turning toward a humane, traditionalist conservatism in response to secular liberalism. Francis Wilson abandoned his liberal ideas because he believed they were based on a faulty understanding of human nature: by ignoring the reality of evil, liberalism dropped moral and political restraints, leading to anarchy and eventually tyranny. A convert to Catholicism, Wilson was an articulate Christian scholar, whose *The Case for Conservatism,* according to one of his students, "remains today as one of the finest statements of conservative principles, particularly as they relate to the American political system." A professor at the University of Illinois for many years, Wilson was a founding editor of *Modern Age.*

The Case for Conservatism; 1951; reprinted, New York, Greenwood Press, 1969; *A Theory of Public Opinion;* 1962; reprinted, New York, Greenwood Press, 1975.

Part III — Current Sources of Conservative Thought

Journals and Periodicals

Access to Energy

Box 2298, Boulder, CO 80306. Annual subscription $22.00. Monthly.

As the title implies, this newsletter supports market-oriented approaches to energy, resources, and the environment, unhampered by the static management of ideological bureaucrats.

AEI Economist

American Enterprise Institute for Public Policy Research, 1150 Seventeenth St., N.W., Washington, DC 20036. Outside Washington, DC: (800) 424-2873; in Washington, DC: (202) 862-5869. Annual subscription $24.00. Monthly.

Edited by Herbert Stein, this newsletter covers a broad range of current economic problems.

AEI Foreign Policy and Defense Review

American Enterprise Institute for Public Policy Research, 1150 Seventeenth St, N.W., Washington, DC 20036. Outside Washington, DC: (800) 424-2873; in Washington, DC: (202) 862-5869. Annual subscription $18.00. Quarterly.

A substantial journal that presents transcripts of AEI panel discussions as well as longer articles. Contributors have included Jeane J. Kirkpatrick, Arthur Burns, Paul Nitze, and Jean-Francois Revel.

The American Spectator (formerly *The Alternative*)

1101 N. Highland, P.O. Box 10448, Arlington, VA 22210. (703) 243-3733. Annual subscription $21.00. Monthly.

Founded by conservative students at Indiana University, *The Alternative,* under the editorship of the brash, liberal-baiting R. Emmett Tyrrell, Jr., became one of America's most exciting conservative magazines. *The American Spectator,* as it is now called, is often associated with the neoconservative movement, and blends satirical comment with longer, more reflective essays on contemporary American culture. With *National Review* and *Commentary,* it is "must" reading for conservatives.

Backgrounder (includes *Issue Bulletin*)

The Heritage Foundation, 214 Massachusetts Ave., N.E., Washington, DC 20002. (202) 546-4400. Annual subscription $75.00.

This series is a steady stream of conservative policy analysis (there are 8-14 *Backgrounders* per month) which stays right on top of the legislative agenda. Well researched, persuasively argued, each *Backgrounder* has an impact on legislators, journalists, and politicos in general. *Issue Bulletin* appears less often, approximately once a month, but is more in-depth.

Benchmark: A Bimonthly Report on the Constitution and the Courts

Rt. 2 Box 93, Cumberland, VA 23040. (804) 492-4922. Annual subscription $18.00.

The journal of the recently founded Center for Judicial Studies, *Benchmark* carries commentary on a wide variety of judicial, constitutional, and ideological issues. This journal is sure to become a source for those who hope to reverse judicial activism, and rescue the Constitution from being turned into a palimpsest.

The Chesterton Review

St. Thomas More College, 1437 College Drive, Saskatoon, Saskatchewan, Canada S7N 0W6. Annual subscription $17.00 Quarterly.

The Chesterton Review is not only an excellent source for thoughtful studies of GKC, but also for reprinted essays and reviews by the Master, and for pieces on his intellectual and social milieu. Recent special issues have focused on Father Brown, Eric Gill, and Christopher Dawson.

Christian Anti-Communism Crusade Newsletter

124 E. First St., Long Beach, CA 90801. (213) 437-0941. Complimentary subscription. Biweekly.

This newsletter covers issues of Communist persecution of Christianity and carries general critiques of Soviet advances around the world.

Chronicles: A Magazine of American Culture (formerly Chronicles of Culture)

934 N. Main St., Rockford, IL 61103. (815) 964-5811. Annual subscription $18.00. Monthly.

The "culture" chronicled in this journal is largely *liberal* culture, and it comes in for relentless attack. Originally a book review magazine, *Chronicles of Culture* now contains essays and many short features, such as film reviews and comments on the journalistic scene. Though occasionally heavy-handed, this magazine is always spirited and readable.

The Claremont Review of Books

The Claremont Institute for the Study of Statesmanship and Political Philosophy, 4650 Arrow Hwy., Suite D-6, Montclair, CA 91763. (714) 621-6825. Annual subscription $10.00. Quarterly.

An outgrowth of the large conservative contingent at Claremont, most of whom are followers of the political philosopher Leo Strauss, this journal is an urbane cultural review. Current issues are seen in the light of larger, philosophical questions, especially the American political tradition established by the Founding Fathers.

Commentary

165 E. 56th St., New York, NY 10022. (212) 751-4000. Annual subscription $33.00. Monthly.

Edited by Norman Podhoretz, *Commentary* is the forum that fostered the growth of the "neoconservative" movement, which first arose among Jewish intellectuals who were responding to the increasingly "soft" position liberal Democrats were taking toward world communism. For sheer power of thought, few journals come close to *Commentary*. Regular contributors include Midge Decter, Peter Berger, Irving Kristol, Ernest van den Haag, and Walter Berns.

Conservative Digest

P.O. Box 2244, Ft. Collins, CO 80522. (800) 847-0122. Annual subscription $19.95. Eleven issues per year.

Conservative Digest was recently taken over and changed into a *Reader's Digest* format, but it still takes its tone from its founder, the New Right direct-mail mogul, Richard Viguerie. Its audience consists of rank-and-file populist conservatives, and its focus is political. In addition to supporting active anti-Communism, strong defense, and the free market, *CD* presses strongly for such social issues as school prayer, pro-life laws, and vouchers for education.

Consumer Research

Education & Research Institute, 517 2nd St., N.E., Washington, DC 20002. (202) 546-1710. Annual subscription $18.00. Monthly.

Very much in the shadow of *Consumer Reports, Consumer Digest* quietly discusses the broad range of consumer issues from a dispassionate, non-ideological standpoint.

Continuity: A Journal of History

Intercollegiate Studies Institute, 14 S. Bryn Mawr Ave., Bryn Mawr, PA 19010. (215) 525-7501. Annual subscription $10.00. Semi-annual.

A scholarly journal that is eminently readable, *Continuity* is a forum for conservative historians whose work has long been suppressed in the professional publications and organizations of a discipline that has been dominated by Marxism, Freudianism, and—more recently—feminism. One of *Continuity*'s strongest points is a section of "Booknotes," containing short, incisive reviews of recent works relating to history. Special issues have touched on the American South, Conservatism and History, and Cultural Continuity.

Crisis: A Journal of Lay Opinion

P.O. Box 495, Notre Dame, IN 46556. (219) 234-3759. Annual subscription $19.95. Monthly.

Founded by Michael Novak and Ralph McInerny, *Crisis (formerly Catholicism in Crisis)* represents a concerted effort by members of the laity to uphold Church teaching against liberals who would politicize the Church and who press for the unraveling of moral theology. Though many of the issues in the journal—the nuclear and economics pastorals, abortion, Church and state conflicts—are political, there is a constant emphasis on the cultural and spiritual heritage of Catholicism.

The Dartmouth Review

P.O. Box 343, Hanover, NH 03755. (603) 643-4370. Annual subscription $25.00. Weekly during semester.

It may not have been the first conservative student newspaper, but *The Dartmouth Review* has become the symbol of a new generation of pugnacious, anti-establishment papers on the liberal-dominated American campuses. Though it is perpetually immersed in controversy, most conservatives seem willing to indulge *The Dartmouth Review*'s occasional excesses. In several instances, the paper's aggressive investigative journalism has revealed a great deal of egg on liberal professorial and administrative faces. For more information about conservative student newspapers, contact the Institute for Educational Affairs, 1112 Sixteenth St., N.W., Suite 1500, Washington, DC 20036; (202) 833-1801.

Dawson Newsletter

P.O. Box 332, Fayetteville, AR 72702. Annual subscription $6.00. Quarterly.

Published by the Society for Christian Culture, this newsletter furthers an appreciation of Catholic historian, Christopher Dawson. Dawson not only was one of the finest historians of the development of Western, Christian Europe, he was also a staunch anti-progressivist who assailed the historicism underlying the liberal ideology.

Education Update

The Heritage Foundation, 214 Massachusetts Ave., N.E., Washington, DC 20002. (202) 546-4400. $8.00. Quarterly.

Another good source of conservative policy analysis, with helpful assessments of legislative initiatives to break the government and union stranglehold on American education.

Enterprise Zone News

Sabre Foundation, 1815 N. Lynn, Suite 200, Arlington, VA 22209. (703) 528-2152. Annual subscription $75.00. Bimonthly.

This newsletter provides important information about Enterprise Zones, both here and abroad.

Family Protection Report

The Child and Family Protection Institute, 721 Second St., N.E., Washington, DC 20002. (202) 546-3004. Annual subscription $25.00. Monthly.

Directed to those who seek to preserve the family from state-sanctioned violence, whether through abortion, infanticide, a weakening of laws protecting children, or other means. Legislative updates, book reviews, interviews, and short articles make up each issue.

Freedom at Issue

Freedom House, 48 E. 21st St., New York, NY 10010. (212) 473-9691. Annual subscription $10.00. Bimonthly.

Freedom House is the organization that tracks the rise or decline of oppression around the world (it publishes a well-known "map" of freedom each year). *Freedom at Issue* is a thoughtful journal exploring these problems in depth. Not a "conservative" journal per se, it nevertheless shuns liberal one-sidedness and freely denounces communist imperialism as well as, say, South African *apartheid* or South American military regimes.

The Freeman

Foundation for Economic Education, Irvington-on-Hudson, NY 10533. (914) 591-7230. Complimentary subscription available. Monthly.

For several decades, *The Freeman* has promoted private property and the free market economy in its short, easily understood essays. Veteran conservative journalist John Chamberlain contributes a book review to every issue.

Government Union Review

Public Service Research Foundation, 8330 Old Courthouse Rd., Suite 600, Vienna, VA 22180. (703) 790-0780. Annual subscription $10.00. Quarterly.

This journal covers labor relations in the public sector.

Harvard Journal of Law and Public Policy

Harvard Law School, Langdell Hall, Cambridge, MA 02138. Annual subscription $22.50. Quarterly.

Another example of how a concentration of conservative students can create the energy for a new publication. In 1978, students at Harvard, frustrated by the lack of legal forums that would air conservative opinions, began publishing essays by major scholars, as well as younger writers.

The Harvard Salient

P.O. Box 1053, Cambridge, MA 02238. (617) 492-0069. Annual subscription $15.00. Bi-weekly during semester.

One of the better conservative student alternative newspapers. Less deliberately controversial than *The Dartmouth Review,* it carries nonetheless pugnacious, closely reasoned editorials and occasionally an "investigative" article.

The Hillsdale Review

P.O. Box 453, Duluth, MN 55806. (218) 525-7167. Annual subscription $10.00. Quarterly.

Founded by conservative students at Hillsdale College, *The Hillsdale Review* is an independent journal of cultural and literary criticism featuring younger writers. One of the few "little reviews" in conservative circles, it probes morals, manners, and art, and contains satire, essays, reviews, and poetry.

Human Events

422 First St., S.E., Washington, DC 20003. (202) 546-0856. Annual subscription $25.00. Weekly.

The granddaddy of weekly conservative journalism, *Human Events* recently celebrated its 40th anniversary. Its appeal is to rank-and-file conservatives, and its strength is a tough conservative perspective on the political scene. Also includes a number of leading conservative columnists.

Human Life Review

150 E. 35th St., Room 840, New York, NY 10016. (212) 685-5210. Annual subscription $15.00. Quarterly.

Covering not just abortion but the whole spectrum of "life" issues, this quarterly features legal, medical, political, philosophical, and even literary articles by such writers as Malcolm Muggeridge, Joseph Sobran, and Francis Canavan, S.J. Each issue provides appendices full of documentation.

Imprimis

Center for Constructive Alternatives, Hillsdale College, Hillsdale, MI 49242. (517) 437-7341. Complimentary subscription available. Monthly.

The essays that make up this series are drawn from the many seminars sponsored by Hillsdale College—the Center for Constructive Alternatives, the Ludwig von Mises Lecture Program, the Shavano Institute—and are by renowned scholars, writers, and public officials. The topics range from theology to economics to art.

Insight

The Washington Times, 3600 New York Ave., N.E., Washington, DC 20002. (800) 336-7666. Complimentary subscription to qualified requesters.

This is an ambitious weekly newsmagazine, roughly modeled on *Time* and *Newsweek,* and published by *The Washington Times.* Like *The Washington Times, Insight* is marked by a conservative editorial stance and the kind of reporting that liberal news journals are not likely to undertake. Also like *The Washington Times, Insight* is read primarily by the Washington political community.

The Intercollegiate Review: A Journal of Scholarship and Opinion

Intercollegiate Studies Institute, 14 S. Bryn Mawr Ave., Bryn Mawr, PA 19010. (215) 525-7501. Complimentary subscriptions available for students and faculty members. Non-academic subscription $10.00. Two to three issues per year.

The Intercollegiate Review is a scholarly, but readable, interdisciplinary journal, covering central topics in political science, history, philosophy, economics, and literature. It probes the cultural, historical, and philosophical forces that lie beneath current issues. Each issue contains information about ISI's many programs and lists books ISI offers at greatly reduced prices.

Interpretation: A Journal of Political Philosophy

Queens College, Flushing, NY 11367. (718) 520-7099. Annual subscription $15.00. Three times a year.

A journal of political theory influenced largely by the teachings of the great philosopher, Leo Strauss. Unlike the majority of the political science profession, dominated by quantitative social science or ideological bias, this journal represents a return to a theoretical approach to political problems.

Lincoln Review

The Lincoln Institute for Research and Education, 1735 DeSales St., N.W., Suite 500, Washington, DC 20036. (202) 347-0872. Annual subscription $12.00. Quarterly.

Though not widely known, *Lincoln Review* represents a significant segment of the black community which refuses liberal panaceas for the problems of minorities. Powered by the economic studies of such black scholars as Walter Williams and

Thomas Sowell, this journal covers public policy issues and cultural trends.

Manhattan Report

Manhattan Institute for Policy Research, 131 Spring St., New York, NY 10012. (212) 219-0773. Annual subscription $12.00. Bi-monthly.

The leitmotif for this report is the free market's creative and productive potential, and each issue deals with innovative policy prescriptions that will restore the marketplace.

Modern Age: A Quarterly Review

Intercollegiate Studies Institute, 14 S. Bryn Mawr Ave., Bryn Mawr, PA 19010. (215) 525-7501. Annual subscription $15.00. Quarterly.

Described by George Nash in his history of the post-war conservative intellectual movement as "the principal quarterly of the intellectual Right." Founded by Russell Kirk in 1957, *Modern Age* contains the finest conservative scholarship in America, and includes a book review section of remarkable depth.

National Review

150 E. 35th St., New York, NY 10016. (212) 679-7330. Annual subscription $34.00. Bi-weekly.

In the national debate, *National Review* has been the leading voice of the conservative mainstream since William F. Buckley, Jr. began publishing in 1955. The primary source of opinion for President Ronald Reagan (among others), *National Review* has always been marked by wit, grace, and—increasingly rare these days—humor. It is, in short, indispensable.

National Security Record

The Heritage Foundation, 214 Massachusetts Ave., N.E., Washington, DC 20002. (202) 546-4400. Annual subscription $50.00. Monthly.

An important source of policy analysis in national security and foreign affairs.

The New Criterion

850 Seventh Ave., New York, NY 10019. (212) 247-6980. Annual subscription $27.00. Monthly with combined July/August and December/January issues.

The New Criterion is a natural outgrowth of the neoconservative movement: a journal of the arts which eschews trendy ideological causes of the culturati, and maintains that standards and a high view of art are crucial for the survival of culture. Edited by Hilton Kramer, former art editor of *The New York Times,* this journal is already, in its third year, required reading for anyone interested in the arts.

New Guard

Young Americans for Freedom, P.O. Box 847, Sierra Madre, CA 91024. (818) 954-9589. Annual subscription $10.00 for non-members. Quarterly.

YAF is the oldest and largest conservative youth group in America, and this journal is geared toward its membership. Calling for less government intervention in the market and a tough anti-Communist foreign policy, *New Guard* is one of the rallying points for the growing conservative student movement.

Orbis: A Journal of World Affairs

Foreign Policy Research Institute, 3508 Market St., Suite 350, Philadelphia, PA 19104. (215) 382-0685. Annual subscription $15.00. Quarterly.

Providing sound scholarship in international affairs, Orbis is consulted by Congressmen, foreign policy officials, and academics. Arms control, U.S.-Soviet relations, and Third World conflicts are frequent topics in this respected journal.

Phyllis Schlafly Report

Box 618, Alton, IL 62002. (618) 462-5415. $10.00. Monthly.

She may be "the sweetheart of the Silent Majority," but Phyllis Schlafly is also a seasoned political actor who intelligently mobilizes the resistance movement to liberalism's anarchic social policy. This newsletter keeps abreast of such issues as the "once and future" Equal Rights Amendment and other family-related policies.

Persuasion at Work

P.O. Box 416, Mount Morris, IL 61054. (815) 964-5811. Annual subscription $18.00. Monthly.

Dealing primarily with social and economic policy, this essay series argues against the counter-productive intrusions of government into business and such institutions as the family and the public schools.

Policy Review

The Heritage Foundation, 214 Massachusetts Ave., N.E., Washington, DC 20002. (202) 546-4400. Annual subscription $15.00. Quarterly.

Less involved with in-depth policy analysis than in its first years of publication, *Policy Review* is turning to a broader range of commentary, especially in dissecting liberalism, and attempts to display the intellectual vigor of conservatism.

The Political Science Reviewer

Intercollegiate Studies Institute, 14 S. Bryn Mawr Ave., Bryn Mawr, PA 19010. (215) 525-7501. Annual subscription $10.00. Annual.

Another conservative renegade in the political science profession, this annual contains long essay-reviews of classic and contemporary works of political science, college textbooks, and Constitutional studies.

Prospect

Concerned Alumni of Princeton, 20 Nassau St., Princeton, NJ 08542. (609) 924-8182. Complimentary subscription available.

Not a student journal, *Prospect* is published by the Concerned Alumni of Princeton, and seeks to be a conservative gadfly in a liberal, and often radical, university. Representative of the conservative revolt in the Ivy League, *Prospect* is considered both controversial and "divisive."

The Public Interest

10 E. 53rd St., New York, NY 10022. (212) 593-7123. Annual subscription $18.00. Quarterly.

Edited by Irving Kristol and Nathan Glazer, *The Public Interest* is the leading neoconservative journal of public policy, and has published many ground-breaking analyses of social, economic, and foreign affairs.

Public Opinion

American Enterprise Institute for Public Policy Research, 1150 Seventeenth St., N.W., Washington, DC 20036. Outside Washington, DC: (800) 424-2873; in Washington, DC: (202) 862-5869. Annual subscription $26.00. Bi-monthly.

In the often murky world of public opinion analysis, this journal seeks rigorous objectivity and extends to larger analyses of the American political process. Interestingly, many of the finest scholars of the formation of opinion and the electoral process have moved toward a neoconservative stance; these include *Public Opinion*'s editors, Seymour Martin Lipset, Ben Wattenberg, and Everett Carll Ladd.

Reason

Box 28897, San Diego, CA 92128. (805) 966-9573. Subscription available only to members of the Reason Foundation: Annual membership $19.50. Monthly.

With the folding of *Inquiry, Reason* may well be the leading magazine of the libertarian movement. Its concerns, while often overlapping with mainstream conservative thought, reflect some of the particular libertarian approaches to such areas as foreign policy and social issues.

The Religion & Society Report

Rockford Institute, Center on Religion & Society, P.O. Box 800, Rockford, IL 61105. (815) 964-5811. Annual subscription $24.00. Monthly.

Editor Richard John Neuhaus is one of the most eloquent neoconservative critics of the politicization of the mainstream Churches, and this newsletter is part of the growing effort to restore balance and a sense of priorities in the religious approach to the political sphere.

The Sewanee Review

University of the South, Sewanee, TN 37375. (615) 598-5931. Annual subscription $12.00. Quarterly.

At a time when literary criticism is being swept away by radical and even nihilistic schools of thought, *The Sewanee Review* maintains a traditional, but inclusive, approach to literature. It has long been associated with Southern conservatism.

The Southern Partisan

P.O. Box 11708, Columbia, SC 29211. (803) 254-3660. Annual subscription $12.00. Quarterly.

Though it indulges in a fair bit of nostalgia, this magazine nonetheless contains a good deal of astringent social commentary, plus interviews and reprintings of classic Southern essays.

The Southern Review

Louisiana State University, 43 Allen Hall, Baton Rouge, LA 70803. (504) 388-1175. Annual subscription $12.00. Quarterly.

Like *The Sewanee Review,* this venerable literary quarterly avoids the winds of doctrine. It also has the tradition of occasionally publishing major essays of political philosophy, including some by Eric Voegelin.

This World

Institute for Educational Affairs/American Enterprise Institute for Public Policy Research, 1112 Sixteenth St., N.W., Suite 1500,

Washington, DC 20036. (202) 547-3191. Annual subscription $16.00. Quarterly.

The primary focus of this journal, co-published by the American Enterprise Institute and the Institute for Educational Affairs, is a non-ideological approach to the relation of religion to the political and economic realms. But it also publishes a wide range of cultural commentary.

Thought: A Review of Culture and Ideas

Fordham University Press, University Box L, Bronx, NY 10458. (212) 579-2320. Annual subscription $15.00. Quarterly.

Nearly 60 years old, *Thought* is "a forum for the discussion of the humanities," including contemporary issues in philosophy, theology, literature, and the arts "within the context of the Judaeo-Christian tradition." Its contributors have included Walker Percy, W.H. Auden, Gabriel Marcel, and Bernard Lonegran.

The University Bookman

P.O. Box 3070, Grand Central Station, New York, NY 10017. Annual subscription $5.00. Quarterly.

Edited by one of the founding fathers of modern conservatism, Russell Kirk, this slim quarterly is devoted primarily to the state of higher education in America. Each issue, however, contains several reviews on a variety of topics, and poetry is also featured.

The Wall Street Journal

200 Burnett Road, Chicopee, MA 01021. Annual subscription $114.00.

In addition to being the world's leading business newspaper, editor Bob Bartley has made the editorial pages of the *Wall Street Journal* the most penetrating, urbane, and principled daily commentary available anywhere.

The Washington Quarterly

MIT Press, Journals Dept., 28 Carlton St., Cambridge MA 02142. Annual subscription $20.00. Quarterly.

Free from ideological muddle, this foreign policy journal is directed toward scholars, businessmen, and government officials.

The Washington Times

3600 New York Ave., N.E., Washington, DC 20002. (202) 636-3000. Daily on weekdays.

A valiant competitor with the obese, liberal in-house newsletter known as *The Washington Post, The Washington Times* provides not only more inches of conservative opinion than any other American newspaper, but reports on events and issues which stand in the liberal blind spot.

The World & I

2850 New York Ave., N.E., Washington, DC 20002. Annual subscription $90.00. Monthly.

Another project of *The Washington Times,* this is a 700-page monthly journal covering news, culture, the arts and sciences, and the intellectual scene. Though it is a formidable volume to read, the sections on books and "modern thought" feature readable and incisive conservative criticism.

The Yale Literary Magazine

Box 243-A Yale Station, New Haven, CT 06520. (203) 624-8400. Annual subscription $28. Occasional.

Purchased for a song by some conservative Yale students, this ancient journal was turned into a journal of the arts, featuring world-class poets and essays on artists accompanied by graphic reproductions that would make Franco Maria Ricci envious. The conservative opinions of the journal caused hysteria among the liberal community at Yale, and a court decision recently denied the magazine's right to use the name "Yale." The case is still in the courts.

Conservatism in Action:
Think Tanks and Foundations

Accuracy in Academia

1275 K St., N.W., Washington, DC 20005. (202) 371-6710.

An offshoot of Reed Irvine's Accuracy in Media, AIA attempts to point out, and presumably correct, ideological bias in university classrooms. It has generated heated controversy, even in conservative circles. AIA operates through students who report on "seriously inaccurate information being imparted by classroom instructors—either through lectures or required reading material." AIA publishes a newsletter, *Campus Report,* which publicizes the cases it investigates.

Accuracy in Media

1275 K St., N.W., Suite 1150, Washington, DC 20005. (202) 371-6710.

Kevin Phillips coined the term "mediacracy," or rule by the media, to describe the presentation and manipulation of opinion today. AIM, a non-partisan group founded in 1969, acts as a watchdog to keep the media honest. It receives complaints from the public, and, if they are justified, asks that the errors be corrected publicly. When such errors are not recanted, AIM publicizes the omissions through *AIM Report.*

Afghanistan Information Center

48 E. 21st. St., New York, NY 10010. (212) 473-9691.

A special project of Freedom House, the Center disseminates information on the current situation in Afghanistan, including Soviet military actions and the efforts of Afghan resistance groups.

American Enterprise Institute

1150 17th St., N.W., Washington, DC 20036. (202) 862-5800.

AEI is one of the largest and most venerable of Washington's think tanks. It publishes several journals and numerous books and pamphlets written by resident scholars. It covers the whole range of public policy issues, sponsors research into Constitutional matters and analyzes the moral and cultural foundations of liberal democracy.

American Family Institute

422 C St., N.E., Washington, DC 20002. (202) 544-1150.

This pro-family organization has published various monographs, including *The Wealth of Families: Ethics and Economics in the 1980s* (1982), with contributions by George Gilder, James L. Buckley, Midge Decter, and others.

American Security Council

Washington Communications Center, Boston, VA 22713. (703) 547-1750.

An umbrella group sponsoring several journals, newsletters, and research institutes, ASC is one of the leading conservative foreign policy organizations. Among its activities is the Coalition for Peace Through Strength—a phrase that would be a good motto for the whole organization.

Campus Coalition for Democracy

C/o Dr. Stephen Balch, P.O. Box 20132, Columbus Circle Station, New York, NY 10023.

The Coalition was "formed to combat the widespread blindness within the academic community to the moral worth of free institutions, and the need to protect them from external threat." CCD seeks to mobilize a broad spectrum of generally conservative professors and graduate students against the disproportionate influence of radicals in the academy. It runs a speakers bureau, publishes a journal, *Academic Questions,* and hosts conferences and seminars on timely issues.

Capital Legal Foundation

700 E St., S.E., Washington, DC 20003. (202) 546-5533.

See entry for the National Legal Center for the Public Trust.

The Cato Institute

224 Second St., S.E., Washington, DC 20003. (202) 546-0200.

Like many libertarian groups, The Cato Institute is well-funded and produces a formidable array of journals, newsletters, and conferences defending the free market and offering public policy initiatives to restore individual freedom. But, like many libertarian groups, its stands on certain social and foreign policy questions are repugnant to conservatives. It has also been associated with the Institute for Policy Studies, a radical foundation of Communist fellow travelers.

Center for Judicial Studies

P.O. Box 15449, Washington, DC 20003.

This newly-founded center is already acting as a clearinghouse for outstanding conservative analysis of current Constitutional and judicial decisions and interpretations. It publishes a journal called *Benchmark,* and has also begun a series of monographs on specific issues such as Federal court involvement in the legalization of homosexual conduct and the failure of modern legal philosophy.

Center for Political Economy and Natural Resources

Montana State University, Bozeman, MT 59719. (406) 994-3871.

One of the most exciting areas of economic study in the last ten years has been in population and natural resources. Much of the innovative study of market solutions to resource problems has been done by scholars associated with this center: Richard Stroup, John Baden, Terry Anderson, and others.

Center for Strategic and International Studies

Georgetown University, 1800 K St., N.W. Washington, DC 20006. (202) 887-0200.

The scholars who make up the CSIS are heavyweights (they include Jeane J. Kirkpatrick and Paul Craig Roberts), and their research in the fields of foreign policy and international economics has provided the Reagan administration with solid, realistic foundations for the formation of policy.

Center for the Study of Market Processes

George Mason University, Dept. of Economics, 4400 University Drive, Fairfax, VA 22030. (703) 323-3483.

The thrust of this program is the study of Austrian economics (the free market school associated with such figures as Ludwig von Mises and Friedrich von Hayek). In addition to research conducted by scholars, courses are offered to students from outside George Mason University.

Center for the Study of Public Choice

George Mason University, St. George's Hall, 4400 University Drive, Fairfax, VA 22030. (703) 323-3770.

The "public choice theory" of economics is causing a quiet revolution in the discipline. Simply stated, this theory sees economic choices in the context of politics: in a democratic welfare state, special interests dominate the legislative process, and politicians respond by accommodating them. The Center has several of the originators of the theory in residence: among them, James Buchanan and Gordon Tullock.

Center on Religion and Society

152 Madison Ave., 24th Floor, New York, NY 10016. (212) 532-4320.

An offshoot of the Rockford Institute, this organization is directed by Richard John Neuhaus, and deals with the increasing domination of mainstream churches by left-wing ideologies. It sponsors conferences and publishes a newsletter, *The Religion and Society Report.*

The Claremont Institute for the Study of Statesmanship and Political Philosophy

4650 Arrow Hwy., Suite D-6, Montclair, CA 91763. (714) 621-6825.

Influenced by the philosopher Leo Strauss, a number of his students formed this institute to further study in political theory

211

and statesmanship. *The Claremont Review of Books* is the Institute's publication.

Committee for the Free World

211 E. 51st St., New York, NY 10022. (212) 759-7737.

Directed by Midge Decter, the Committee for the Free World has gathered the support of dozens of influential scholars, writers, and public figures from around the world (including, for example, English playwright Tom Stoppard and American novelist Saul Bellow) in an effort to oppose Soviet expansionism and bolster the Western military and diplomatic response.

Committee for Monetary Research & Education

P.O. Box 1630, Greenwich, CT 06830. (203) 661-2533.

CMRE is an educational foundation which supports the gold standard and other measures to ensure that a healthy monetary system supports the free society.

Committee for the Survival of a Free Congress

721 Second St., N.E., Washington, DC 20002. (202) 546-3000.

A bi-partisan political action committee dedicated to the election of "conservative, responsible, and realistic leaders" to the U.S. Congress. In addition to a variety of political activities, such as training candidates and campaign personnel, the Committee publishes newsletters and books. Like other New Right groups, there is a strong emphasis on social and family-related issues.

Committee on the Present Danger

905 16th St., N.W., Suite 207, Washington, DC 20006. (202) 628-2409.

A non-profit, non-partisan organization promoting better understanding of the problems confronting foreign policy. Its "main premise is that the U.S. must increase defense spending and modernize weapons systems to meet growing Soviet military strength."

Eagle Forum

Box 618, Alton, IL 62002. (618) 462-5415.

Phyllis Schlafly's band of men and women dedicated to protecting traditional Christian morals and institutions. It fights "against forces that are anti-family, anti-religious, anti-morality, anti-children, anti-life, and anti-self defense."

Education & Research Institute

517 2nd St., N.E., Washington, DC 20002. (202) 546-1710.

Together with the National Journalism Center, ERI works to develop young conservative writers. It has regular student interns and sponsors conferences and workshops.

Educational Research Council of America

Rockefeller Bldg., 614 Superior Ave. West, Cleveland, OH 44113. (216) 696-8222.

For many years, ERCA has produced elementary and high school textbooks that are free from the slanted interpretations of the liberal *Zeitgeist*. Russell Kirk has long been associated with this group, and has produced several texts himself.

Ethics and Public Policy Center

1030 Fifteenth St., N.W., Suite 300, Washington, DC 20005. (202) 682-1200.

As the 1984 elections confirmed, religion and politics are now more inextricably bound up in America than ever before, especially as liberalism, which has demonstrably failed at the level of ideas and public policy, relies more heavily on the "politics of compassion" to bolster its case. The Ethics and Public Policy Center is one of few places where clarity and an emphasis on traditional Judeo-Christian mores (such as respect for the individual, the rule of law, and limited government) is applied to many of the issues which liberals have sought to monopolize. The Center produces a steady stream of timely books, essays, and conference proceedings on topics like liberation theology, the World Council of Churches, South Africa, and nuclear arms.

The Federalist Society for Law & Public Policy Studies

1625 Eye St., N.W., Washington, DC 20006. (202) 822-8138.

Working through many of the nation's leading law schools, the Federalist Society promotes the principles "that the state exists to preserve freedom, that the separation of powers is central to the American Constitution, and that it is emphatically the province and duty of the judiciary to say what the law *is,* not what it should *be."* Among its activities are major conferences which "focus attention on areas of the law in which the liberal orthodoxy is particularly in need of re-examination."

Fisher Institute

6350 LBJ Freeway, Suite 183E, Dallas, TX 75240. (214) 233-1041.

A pro-free market organization that publishes intelligent studies on vital issues of public policy.

Foreign Policy Research Institute

3508 Market St., Suite 350, Philadelphia, PA 19104. (215) 382-0685.

FPRI is one of the leading conservative foreign policy research centers. In addition to its quarterly journal, *Orbis,* FPRI publishes a distinguished series of *Philadelphia Policy Papers* (really books) on such subjects as the War Powers Act, the politics of the nuclear freeze, and nuclear strategy.

Foundation for Economic Education

Irvington-on-Hudson, NY 10533. (914) 591-7230.

For four decades, FEE has championed the free market, private property, and limited government. Truly an educational organization, FEE sponsors numerous seminars around the country and publishes *The Freeman.* Some of the leading free market scholars—Ludwig von Mises among them—have been associated with FEE. Staff members also specialize in providing information on books and other materials for classroom use in schools and universities.

Freedom House

48 E. 21st St., New York, NY 10010. (212) 473-9691.

While not strictly a "conservative organization," Freedom House, with its focus on the extent of freedom in the nations of the world, approaches the question of oppression in a non-ideological fashion, exposing Communist totalitarianism as well as military dictatorships. It is thus largely free from the liberal cant that refuses to see enemies to the Left. It holds frequent press conferences on current issues, such as one recent conference featuring defectors from the Soviet army in Afghanistan.

Freedom's Foundation at Valley Forge

P.O. Box 706, Rt. 23, Valley Forge, PA 19481. (215) 933-8825.

A non-political, non-sectarian educational organization, the Freedom's Foundation makes awards to outstanding conservative journalists and groups. It also occasionally holds conferences.

Gulf Coast & Great Plains Legal Foundation

101 W. 11th St., Suite 1000, Kansas City, MO 64105. (816) 474-6600.

See entry for the National Legal Center for the Public Trust.

The Heritage Foundation

214 Massachusetts Ave., N.E., Washington, DC 20002. (202) 546-4400.

Quite simply, the Heritage Foundation is the largest, most creative and energetic conservative public policy think tank in America. Perhaps its greatest claim to fame is its ability to produce sophisticated, well-documented policy analyses (*Issue Bulletins* and *Backgrounders*) with a swiftness that makes them timely and thus influential. It is no secret that President Reagan relies on such Heritage policy prescriptions as the *Mandate for Leadership* series, and Heritage staff members often take government or congressional posts. Heritage's array of publications include *Policy Review, Policy Digest, Insider's Newsletter, Education Update,* and *National Security Record.* It sponsors lectures and conferences regularly, nearly all of which are later published. Its Resource Bank is a mine of information about conservative public policy experts and conservative studies and meetings. An internship program also brings students to Washington and provides them with first-hand experience of Congress and the legislative process.

The Hoover Institution on War, Revolution and Peace

Stanford University, Stanford, CA 94305. (415) 497-1754.

Similar to the Heritage Foundation in size, intellectual power, and breadth of policy analysis, the Hoover Institution is more geared to advanced, interdisciplinary scholarship. Hoover's Senior Fellows number among them some of the finest conservative minds, such as Martin Anderson, Thomas Sowell, and Milton Friedman. Many of Hoover's scholars have held high government positions, and they often provide expert congressional testimony. The Hoover Institution Press publishes dozens of books on both international and domestic issues.

Hudson Institute

620 Union Dr., P.O. Box 648, Indianapolis, IN 46206. (317) 632-1787.

Long associated with the late Herman Kahn, the Hudson Institute conducts studies affecting corporate and government planning, all from a non-liberal perspective.

Institute for Contemporary Studies

785 Market St., Suite 750, San Francisco, CA 94103. (415) 543-6213.

A public policy research organization, ICS specializes in book-length studies that demonstrate the free market's superior performance when compared to government intervention in business. But it also ranges beyond domestic policy, as in its recent publication of *The Grenada Papers,* the documents revealing the Soviet plans for making Grenada a base for Communist imperialism in the Caribbean. ICS also sponsors the "Midnight Economist" radio broadcasts of Dr. William Allen.

Institute for Educational Affairs

1112 16th St., N.W., Suite 1500, Washington, DC 20036. (202) 833-1801.

IEA serves as a clearinghouse for conservative grant-making organizations, providing evaluations of worthy non-profit foundations or projects and channeling support to them. It has also played an important role in fostering the rapid growth of conservative student journalism on the American campuses. IEA co-publishes *This World* with the American Enterprise Institute.

Institute for Foreign Policy Analysis

675 Massachusetts Ave., 10th Floor, Cambridge, MA 02139. (617) 492-2116.

Another outstanding foreign policy think tank, the Institute supports scholarship and publishes a number of monographs on such subjects as arms control, Marxist-Leninist organizations, and the Catholic bishops' pastoral on war and peace.

Institute for Humane Studies

George Mason University, Tallwood House, 4210 Roberts Rd., Fairfax, VA 22030. (703) 323-1055.

Libertarian in its intellectual inspiration, the Institute for Humane Studies was founded to encourage research and advanced study for the strengthening of a free society. Through seminars, fellowships, and publications, IHS has assisted students and younger scholars to develop their thought and establish their professional credentials.

Institute for Research on the Economics of Taxation

1725 K St., N.W., Suite 1103, Washington, DC 20006. (202) 223-6316.

IRET sponsors research, provides publications, and holds seminars to further a knowledge of supply-side economics and its current (or potential) impact on public policy. It publishes *Economic Reports*, a series of studies on tax and fiscal policies, and *Fiscal Issues*, produced jointly with the Heritage Foundation.

Institute on Religion and Democracy

729 15th St., N.W., Suite 900, Washington, DC 20005. (202) 393-3200.

An interdenominational organization, the Institute represents a diversity of theological viewpoints, and upholds the link between Christianity and democracy. Its research, seminars, and publications combat the leftist presence in the churches, as for instance in liberation theology. The Institute believes that democratic capitalism is consistent with Christian moral principles.

Intercollegiate Studies Institute

14 S. Bryn Mawr Ave., Bryn Mawr, PA 19010. (215) 525-7501.

ISI is the pre-eminent conservative intellectual foundation working directly with students and professors in American colleges and universities. Since 1953, ISI has provided a conservative alternative to the prevailing liberal orthodoxy on the campuses through its lectures, conferences, publications, and fellowships. Believing in the integration of knowledge, ISI has fostered an interdisciplinary approach to education. Regional directors work with students and faculty to arrange lectures and seminars, and to distribute literature. ISI's membership totals 30,000 and includes many people outside of academic circles. Its publications include *The Intercollegiate Review, Modern Age, The Political Science Reviewer,* and *Continuity.* ISI also makes available to its members conservative books at drastically reduced prices.

Law and Economics Center

University of Miami, P.O. Box 248000, Coral Gables, FL 33124. (305) 284-6174.

Defending private property and market economics as most conducive to freedom and prosperity, LEC works to educate teachers through intensive "Teaching Institutes" and seminars.

LEARN, Inc.

655 Fifteenth St., N.W., Suite 310, Washington, DC 20005. (202) 639-4525.

LEARN, Inc. is a policy analysis and lobbying organization promoting excellence in education. It publishes studies and supports legislation—such as tuition tax credits and vouchers—that encourages freedom of choice, less intervention by the federal government, and traditional standards of moral and intellectual development.

Liberty Fund

7440 North Shadeland, Indianapolis, IN 46250. (317) 842-0880.

Founded in 1962, the Liberty Fund is known primarily for its book publishing wing, Liberty Press/Liberty Classics, which produces inexpensive, handsomely bound classic and contemporary works on the free society. But the Fund has also sponsored many conferences for conservative and libertarian scholars that have furthered the coherence and insight of conservative analysis.

Lincoln Institute for Research and Education

1735 DeSales St., N.W., Suite 500, Washington, DC 20036. (202) 347-0872.

The Lincoln Institute was founded to study the social, economic, and political issues affecting black America, and to provide an alternative voice on those issues. The Institute has argued that many of the welfare, civil rights, and other programs aimed at helping disadvantaged minorities have been counter-productive. Associated with such outstanding black scholars as Walter Williams and Thomas Sowell, the Institute publishes a quarterly, *The Lincoln Review.*

Manhattan Institute for Policy Research

131 Spring St., New York, NY 10012. (212) 219-0773.

This group is one of the more successful free market policy institutes in gaining media and governmental attention—largely due to its articulate and innovative approaches to public policy. George Gilder, Warren Brookes, and Thomas Sowell are among the writers the Manhattan Institute has brought to a larger public. It publishes a newsletter, *The Manhattan Report,* and holds a number of policy forums, bringing scholars, journalists, and public officials together.

The Media Institute

3017 M St., N.W., Washington, DC 20007. (202) 298-7512.

Some of the studies undertaken by the Media Institute have broken new ground in documenting the liberal bias of the news media, as well as the media's impact on current events. Several of the studies have focused on the evening news, but others have turned to so-called "investigative" and "advocacy" journalism, and the portrayal of businessmen on TV entertainment shows.

Mid-America Legal Foundation

20 N. Wacker Dr., Suite 842, Chicago, IL 60606. (312) 263-5163.

See entry for the National Legal Center for the Public Trust.

Mid-Atlantic Legal Foundation

400 Market St., 3rd Floor, Philadelphia, PA 19106. (215) 238-1367.

See entry for the National Legal Center for the Public Trust.

Moral Majority

Liberty Federation, 305 6th St., Lynchburg, VA 24504. (804) 528-5000.

Perhaps the best known of the religious New Right groups, thanks to its controversial, but shrewd and articulate leader, the Rev. Jerry Falwell, Moral Majority's premise is that a liberal, secular elite is exercising disproportionate control over American social policy, and that the mainstream American citizen should make his essentially conservative ideas known. MM publishes a newspaper and lobbies Congress.

Mountain States Legal Foundation

1200 Lincoln, Suite 600, Denver, CO 80203. (303) 861-0244.

See entry for the National Legal Center for the Public Trust

National Association of Manufacturers

1776 F St., N.W., Washington, DC 20006. (202) 637-3000.

One of the oldest and largest business associations, the NAM has for many years defended the free market through employee education programs, seminars for business leaders, and its journal, *Enterprise.*

National Captive Nation's Committee

P.O. Box 1171, Washington, DC 20013.

The committee "conducts research and disseminates information on captive nations in Central and Eastern Europe, and those within the USSR and the Caribbean." It "acts as a coordinator for many state and local groups and international organizations, and distributes books on captive nations."

National Federation of Independent Business

600 Maryland Ave., S.W., Suite 695, Washington, DC 20024. (202) 554-9000.

Like the NAM, NFIB has been active in employee economic education and lobbying efforts in Washington. It has produced and distributed pro-free market material to a large audience.

National Journalism Center

517 2nd St., N.E., Washington, DC 20002. (202) 546-1710.

Under the directorship of veteran conservative journalist, M. Stanton Evans, the NJC has become a professional training ground for *young* conservative journalists. Students come for a semester and receive training in journalistic techniques, and attend meetings at which leading columnists and public officials speak on current issues. The students then spend a period working as an intern for a wire agency, columnist, magazine, or newspaper, gaining valuable on-the-job experience. The NJC is sure to have a long-term impact on the quality of reporting in the major media.

National Legal Center for the Public Trust

1000 16th St., N.W., Suite 301, Washington, DC 20036. (202) 296-1683.

The umbrella organization for several regional groups, NLCPT engages in research and advocacy, defending traditional American institutions, such as the free enterprise system and private property, from attack in the courts. NLCPT "acts as a resource center, coordinator, and Washington counsel to the regional foundations; publishes a variety of periodicals and other publications; and undertakes educational activities."

National Right to Work Legal Defense Foundation

8001 Braddock Rd., Suite 600, Springfield, VA 22160. (703) 321-8510.

While the big-news labor disputes are always guaranteed public attention, many of the smaller, less attractive features of labor unions escape public scrutiny. The problems of the "closed shop," where individuals are forced to join unions, are the concern of the National Right to Work Legal Defense Foundation, which defends individual cases and seeks to promote a national consensus on the fundamental right to work.

National Strategy Information Center

150 E. 58th St., New York, NY 10155. (212) 838-2912.

A foreign policy think tank that publishes monographs on a variety of contemporary issues.

Pacific Institute for Public Policy Research

177 Post St., San Francisco, CA 94108. (415) 989-0833.

An energetic domestic policy analysis outfit, the Pacific Institute specializes in book-length essay collections on the effects of government intervention in the marketplace. Some of the topics covered are the public schools, public vs. private land use, housing policy, and rights vs. regulations.

Pacific Legal Foundation

555 Capital Mall, Suite 350, Sacramento, CA 95814. (916) 444-0154.

Like other conservative legal foundations, Pacific attempts to combat ideological, anti-private property, anti-individual rights legislation.

The Philadelphia Society

North Adams, MI 49262. (517) 287-5814.

A national association of conservative scholars, businessmen, and activists, the Philadelphia Society holds its annual national meeting in Chicago (it's called "Philadelphia" in memory of the Founding Fathers), and occasional regional meetings around the country. Membership is by invitation only.

Public Research, Syndicated

4650 Arrow Hwy., Suite D-6, Montclair, CA 91763. (714) 621-5831.

PRS is an opinion editorial syndicate, reaching hundreds of college, community, and metropolitan newspapers with conservative viewpoints on current issues.

Reason Foundation

1018 Garden St., Santa Barbara, CA 93101. (805) 963-5993.

A libertarian organization which emphasizes a philosophical approach to the defense of the free society in addition to its public policy studies. It sponsors interdisciplinary conferences, publishes a lively magazine, *Reason,* and an annual essay collection, *Reason Papers.*

Rockford Institute

934 N. Main St., Rockford, IL 61103. (815) 964-5053.

One of the few conservative groups that concentrates on underlying cultural forces instead of public policy, the Rockford Institute has published books on the family, the media, and on the defense of freedom. Its monthly journal is *Chronicles,* a magazine that dissects contemporary liberalism. It also publishes *Persuasion at Work,* a newsletter on social issues sent out to businessmen, public officials, and the general public.

USIC Educational Foundation

220 National Press Bldg., 14th and F Streets, N.W., Washington, DC 20045. (202) 662-8755.

Devoted to defending free enterprise, the USIC Educational Foundation provides opinion editorials to 300 newspapers, and supplies five-minute radio broadcasts to 100 stations, distributes literature, and maintains a speakers bureau. It has also recently developed a program to aid the conservative alternative student newspapers that have sprung up on the campuses.

Young Americans for Freedom

P.O. Box 847, Sierra Madre, CA 91024. (818) 954-9589.

Founded at the home of the Buckleys, YAF is the major conservative political youth organization. It has chapters nationwide, and campaigns for local and national conservative candidates. It publishes *New Guard.*

Young America's Foundation

11800 Sunrise Valley Drive, Suite 812, Reston, VA 22091. (703) 620-5270.

An educational foundation that works with high school seniors and undergraduates, Young America's Foundation holds summer "conservative orientation seminars," to give students a perspective on the issues they are not likely to get from the average professor. It also publishes studies of textbooks, and makes conservative books available to members at reduced prices.

World Research, Incorporated

11722 Sorrento Valley Road, San Diego, CA 92121. (619) 566-3456.

WRI specializes in imaginative audio-visual, educational tools to promote the principles of the free market to students and teachers. It produced the well-known film *The Incredible Bread Machine,* and now has several others on specific subjects.

Conservative Publishers

Basic Books, Inc.

10 E. 53rd St., New York, NY 10022. (212) 593-7057.

Long known as the publishing house of the neoconservatives, Basic Books specializes in major works of public policy that challenge liberal orthodoxy. Among its distinguished authors are Thomas Sowell, Walter Berns, James Q. Wilson, Ernest van den Haag, and Edward Banfield.

Carolina Academic Press

Box 8795, 1003 Chapel Hill St., Durham, NC 27707. (919) 688-5155.

This press has connections with Straussian political philosophers, and publishes works by Harry Jaffa, Francis Canavan, S.J., and others on political theory, history, and literature.

Conservative Book Club

15 Oakland Ave., Harrison, NY 10528. (914) 835-0900.

A major institution in the conservative world, the CBC used to be connected to Arlington House publishers. Now it functions independently, offering many of the best current conservative books at reduced prices.

229

Devin-Adair Company

6 N. Water St., Greenwich, CT 06830. (203) 531-7755.

One of the older conservative publishers, Devin-Adair offers several pungent anti-liberal critiques each year on such subjects as public education, the federal bureaucracy, and the constricted free market economy.

Green Hill Publishers

Box 738, Ottawa, IL 61350. (815) 434-7905.

Among Green Hill's books are various broadsides and manifestoes from politicians of the Right, such as Philip Crane and Guy Vander Jagt. It also prints polemics on bureaucratic waste, regulatory inefficiency, and the communist threat.

Hillsdale College Press

Hillsdale College, Hillsdale, MI 49242. (517) 437-7341.

The books of Hillsdale College President, George C. Roche III are available, as well as the *Champions of Freedom* series, an annual collection of the talks given at the College's Ludwig von Mises Lecture Program.

Hoover Institution Press

Stanford University, Stanford, CA 94305. (415) 497-3373.

HIP produces a wide range of policy analyses in economics, international affairs, communist studies, and domestic politics. The authors are largely drawn from Hoover Institution Fellows, and the research and scholarship is thoroughly documented. HIP also publishes a number of yearbooks about the Soviet Union and other totalitarian nations.

Ignatius Press

P.O. Box 18990, San Francisco, CA 94118.

Ignatius Press specializes in books by outstanding orthodox Roman Catholic theologians of the twentieth century. Many of these writers are not well known even among traditional Catholics: they include Hans Urs von Balthasar, Joseph Cardinal Ratzinger, Louis Bouyer, and Henri de Lubac. In addition, Ignatius puts out books by American Catholic writers like James Hitchcock and James V. Schall, S.J. Also published are anti-liberal books on social issues, each of which is solidly based on Church teaching.

Liberty Press/Liberty Classics

7440 N. Shadeland Ave., Indianapolis, IN 46250. (317) 842-0880.

Liberty Press publishes contemporary works by libertarians and conservatives, including F.A. Hayek, Ludwig von Mises, and W.H. Hutt. Liberty Classics reissues seminal volumes of classical liberal or traditionalist thought in well-edited versions: Adam Smith, David Hume, James Fenimore Cooper, Sir Henry Maine, and Fisher Ames are among the pantheon. Each Liberty Press/Classics book is impeccably bound and printed, and they are available at affordable prices.

Louisiana State University Press

Baton Rouge, LA 70803.

LSU Press carries on the Southern traditional worldview in literary and political works, many of which deal with such anti-liberal writers as Flannery O'Connor, William Faulkner, and Walker Percy. It publishes the works of philosopher Eric Voegelin and other conservative political theorists.

Open Court Publishing Company

1058 Eighth St., Box 599, La Salle, IL 61301. (815) 223-2520.

Has a tradition of publishing philosophical books not necessarily related to conservatism, but regularly puts out conservative books for the general reader, such as Arnold Beichman's
Nine Lies About America and Henri Lepage's *Tomorrow, Capitalism.*

Regnery/Books
A Division of Regnery Gateway, Inc.

700 E. Street, S.E., Washington, DC 20003. (202) 544-6262.

Henry Regnery began publishing books in 1947, and presides
over the most distinguished conservative press in America. His
son, Alfred, is Publisher. From Russell Kirk's *The Conservative
Mind* to the present, Regnery has offered both seminal studies
and timely polemics. Under the "Gateway" series, Regnery
publishes many classics of politics, philosophy, and theology
(Plato, St. Augustine, Aquinas, and more).

Sherwood Sugden Company

1117 Eighth St., La Salle, IL 61301. (815) 223-1231.

A small publisher specializing in philosophical, theological,
and literary works informed by Christian orthodoxy and traditional principles. Authors include M.E. Bradford, Christopher
Dawson, Stanley L. Jaki, Marion Montgomery, and Frederick
Wilhelmsen.

University Press of America

4720 Boston Way, Lanham, MD 20706. (301) 459-3366.

UPA, which specializes in small press run scholarly works, publishes over 400 books a year covering a wide range of subjects. Many of these publications are by conservative professors, and several conservative organizations publish their books through UPA.

Collections of Private Papers

William F. Buckley, Jr. Papers

Historical Manuscripts and Archives Department, Sterling Library, Yale University, New Haven, CT 06540. (203) 436-8335.

William Henry Chamberlin Papers

Providence College Library, Providence, RI 02918. (401) 865-2242.

Donald Davidson Papers

Joint University Libraries, 419 21st Ave. South, Nashville, TN 37420.

Milton Friedman Papers

Hoover Institution Archives, Stanford University, Stanford, CA 94305. (415) 497-2300.

Herbert Hoover Presidential Library

P.O. Box 488, West Branch, IA 52358. (319) 643-5301.

Russell Kirk Papers

Clarke Historical Library, Park 409, Central Michigan University, Mount Pleasant, MI 48859. (517) 774-3352.

Marvin Liebman Papers

Hoover Institution Archives (address as above).

Henry Regnery Papers

Hoover Institution Archives (address as above).

Ralph de Toledano Papers

Hoover Institution Archives (address as above).

Eric Voegelin Papers (partial collection)

Hoover Institution Archives (address as above).

Richard M. Weaver Papers

Joint University Libraries, 419 21st Ave. South, Nashville, TN 37420. (615) 322-2800.

Francis G. Wilson Papers

University Archives, Main Library, 1408 W. Gregory Ave., University of Illinois, Urbana, IL 61801. (217) 333-2290.

Index of Names